Pathways in Juggling

LEARN HOW TO JUGGLE WITH BALLS, CLUBS, DEVIL STICKS, DIABOLOS, AND BEYOND

Robert Irving and Mike Martins

Pathways in Juggling

LEARN HOW TO JUGGLE WITH BALLS, CLUBS, DEVIL STICKS, DIABOLOS, AND BEYOND

Robert Irving and Mike Martins

FIREFLY BOOKS

A FIREFLY BOOK

Published in Canada by
Firefly Books Ltd.
3680 Victoria Park Avenue,
Willowdale, Ontario M2H 3K1

Published in the United States by
Firefly Books (U.S.) Inc.
P.O. Box 1338, Ellicott Station
Buffalo, New York 14205

Cataloguing in Publication Data
Irving, Robert
Pathways in juggling: learn how to juggle with balls, clubs, devil
sticks, diabolos, and beyond
ISBN 1-55209-121-X

1. Juggling Juvenile literature. I. Martins, Mike. II. Title.
GV1558.I78 1997 j793.8'7 C97-930882-8

This book was designed and produced by
Quintet Publishing Limited.
6 Blundell Street, London N7 9BH

Creative Director: Richard Dewing
Design: deep design
Project Editors: Diana Steedman, Doreen Palamartschuk
Editor: Mike Foxwell
Photographer: Jeremy Thomas
Typeset in Great Britain by Type Technique, London W1
Manufactured in Singapore by Universal Graphics Pte Ltd
Printed in Singapore by Star Standard Industries Pte Ltd

CONTENTS

INTRODUCTION 7

1. THREE BALLS 9
The Three-ball Cascade
(or How to Juggle) 9
Over the Top 15
Columns 16
Rainbow Cross 18
Three-ball Shower 20
Stance and Tips 21

2. CLUBS 23
Club Control: Spins and Height 32
Basic Club Tricks 35
Under the Leg 35
Two In One Hand 36
Columns and One-up, Two-up 37
The Helicopter 38
The Club Kick-up 39
Advanced Club Tricks 40
The Three-club Flash 40
Tomahawks 42
Balancing 44
Back Cross 46
Between the Legs 47
Side Spins 48

3. THE NUMBERS GAME 50
Four Balls 50
Half-Shower 52
Five Balls 54
Three-ball Flash 54
The Snake 55
Five Balls 56
Half-Shower 58
Multiplex 59
Five-ball Columns 60

More Clubs	61
Four Clubs	61
Four-Club Half-Shower	63
Five Clubs	64
4. MORE BALLS THAN MOST	65
Three In One Hand	65
Column Variations	67
Figure of Eight variation	68
Over the Top variation	69
The Box	70
Multiplexing and Gathering	72
Dummy Elevator and Variations	74
The Machine	76
Snatching or Clawing	78
Body Bouncing	79
Mill's Mess	81
5. STEALING AND PASSING	86
The Basic Club Pass	87
Five-club Passing	91
Six-club Passing	93
Passing Techniques and Tricks	95
Under the Leg	96
Through the Legs	96
Double-Spin Passes	97
Triple-Spin Passes	98
Torpedo Throws (or Zero Spin)	99
Passing With More Than Two People	100
6. OTHER JUGGLING ITEMS	101
Devil Sticks	101
Spins and Double Spins	104
Windmill	105
Whirlpool Spins	106
Single Sticking	107
Under the Leg	107
Behind the Back	108
The Diabolo	109
Fast Spinning	113
Around the World	114
Foot Tapper	115
Reverse/Cross Catch	116
Cat's Cradle	117
Monkey Climb	118
High Wire	119
Flash Finish	120
7. EQUIPMENT	121
Balls	121
Clubs	122
Devil Sticks	123
Diabolos	124
Fire Products	124
Anything Else At All	125
8. PERFORMING	126
The Authors	128
Acknowledgements	128

Introduction

Juggling is a very special activity. We hesitate to use the word "skill" as the basic three-ball cascade is about as difficult to learn as is tying shoelaces and can be taught to young and old alike. Yet the enjoyment from this uncomplicated activity is without doubt out of all proportion to the level of difficulty. For onlookers it is also incredibly impressive – even with only the very basic three balls. This book is about how to juggle, how to have a lot of fun, and how to look incredibly impressive.

When we discussed the nature of this book, we decided that what was needed was not only how to tell you how to do something, but also to show you. This is a very visual book, something for which we have adopted the phrase "virtual video." We hope you will find it has attributes of both a book that can be used as a source of reference and a video that permits you to see how something should look as well as being told how to do it.

Juggling has permeated history, from the earliest records over 4,000 years ago, which showed that the Egyptians had developed this form of entertainment, through the Middle Ages, which defined the accepted look of a "jester," to modern times where no circus or visual performance is complete without at least one exponent of this art. And art it certainly is, although juggling is a unique activity in that, in learning it, it is the left side of the brain that works through the logical processes of how it all fits together, but it is the right side that finally takes over. Once this transference has taken place – and only when this happens – you can juggle without thinking about it and the artist in you can really get going. Most modern activities do not lend themselves to right-brain thinking, which makes juggling the unusual activity it is.

Juggling is a relaxing activity which can be used as a form of stress relief. Due to the actions necessary, it also gives much-needed movement to the neck and upper torso for those in sedentary jobs. It is also good for the eyes – they need exercise too!

But – you have learned the three-ball cascade. What now? All your friends have been impressed but you have reached the stage where you are looking up old friends to whom you haven't yet shown your new-found skill (there we go again, sorry – "activity"). And isn't it difficult to bring up the subject of juggling when you haven't yet asked about their girlfriend, job, or latest hobby? Or maybe you just feel there are greater challenges in life. There are – and more importantly for you, some of them relate to juggling. This is also what this book is about: what shall I do next, now that I can juggle?

In juggling, as in life, choices are there to be made. These are not necessarily exclusive but humankind has found that specialization leads naturally to greater skill within that specialization. So it is with juggling. We have identified the major paths available to you, once you have mastered basic juggling – although we are not saying that these are the only ones available, or that you should decide to do just one.

 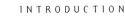

If balls are impressive, a solid-looking, weighty and highly decorated club, spinning and whirling through the air, is vastly more so. So the first path is to look beyond balls at the myriad options available in club juggling, starting with the basics, giving you some pointers in practicing club control, and then giving some practical tricks which can be used to both practice the skills you have learned and to utilize those skills in visually stimulating club juggling tricks.

But while juggling three of anything can be made to look more impressive than it really is, adding additional quantities of balls (or clubs) makes even the most basic pattern stunning. The second pathway is therefore to look into the realm of quantity juggling, the additional timing skills required and the patterns needed to juggle four, five, and more.

Many, many jugglers are in love with three balls. And the patterns that can be performed with just three balls are innumerable. The third pathway is concerned with some of the ways in which the basic three-ball cascade can be enhanced – culminating (in this book at least) with the incredibly visual Mill's Mess.

And then, juggling is a joyous activity – so why not share it? Juggling with a friend, passing and sharing the experience, is not only one of the truly rewarding ways of spending time, but also a massively entertaining spectacle. In Chapter 5 we introduce the basics of these skills, imparting some of the intricacies of timing and the patterns commonly used.

No juggling book would be complete without some reference to the many different types of equipment that can be juggled other than balls and clubs. A couple of hundred years ago the Western world was introduced by the Chinese to the Devil Stick and the Diabolo. In addition to using standard items, many jugglers become avid pyromaniacs, setting fire to anything they can lay their hands on, so we also include a small section on fire products and safety.

And finally, "performance" is the watchword of most jugglers – amateur and professional alike – so we have included a section on the development of routines, "business" to be included therein, and those vitally important aspects: the beginning and the end of a routine.

The enjoyment you derive is a personal experience. Only you can determine which of the above paths you want to tread. So try them all, and above all – have fun!

CHAPTER 1

Three balls

This book is aimed squarely at anyone who wants to, or can, juggle. If you are the latter then this chapter is optional as it deals with how to juggle the basic three-ball cascade, which is the foundation of all juggling. At the end of the chapter are some simple three-ball tricks.

For those of you still with us, this is the beginning. You need to find a little peace and quiet and follow each stage of the process methodically. Go on to the next step when you have successfully managed the previous step at least three times in a row. At any time, if you hit a problem then go back to the previous step and practice again. Juggling is like any complex problem – it can be easily solved by the simple expedient of converting the big problem into smaller, more manageable ones. Each step we take you through is designed to be easily taken so long as the previous one has been well practiced, so do not be afraid to step back once in a while and practice an earlier stage a little more.

First of all, you will need something to juggle with. In Chapter 7 we show some of the different types of juggling ball, but for the beginner we recommend the soft, squidgy type known as "thuds." These have a nice feel to them and tend to stay put when they drop. Alternatively, beanbags of almost any description make excellent material or, in desperation, make your own – a couple of pieces of material sewn together and filled with 3–3½ oz of rice will make do until you get to the store.

We do not recommend scarves, as the timing is peculiar to these items, and moving on to the balls or other weightier objects is as difficult as learning properly in the first place. Neither, for myriad other reasons do we recommend any of the following:

- tennis balls
- fruit of any description
- eggs
- china or glass objects.

The Three-ball Cascade
(or, How to Juggle)

The stance. Determine which is your strong hand and which your weak. Generally if you are right-handed, your left hand will be your weak one. The basic stance of the three-ball cascade is to start with two balls in your weak hand and one in the other. But to begin, throw away two of the balls and let's concentrate on the throw.

The Three-ball Cascade (or, How to Juggle)

2 Take one ball in your weak hand and, using a a sweeping motion inward past your midriff, throw in an arc to your other (strong) hand. Aim for the top of the arc to be on a level with your eyes. As you throw, say "Throw" out loud and as you catch, say "Catch."

3 Do the same starting with your strong hand and catching with your weak hand. Remember to say "Throw" as you throw and "Catch" as you catch. Practice both these steps for several minutes until you are throwing at the same height with both hands.

4 You will find it helps here to imagine a box in front of you with its top level six inches above your head and its base at hand level. All your juggling will take place within the confines of this box. You should aim each of your throws to peak somewhere around the corner of the box. Note that, by moving your hand inward before you throw, each throw is from around your midriff to your shoulder.

Key Stage

5 This is a critical step, so stay calm and relaxed and take your time over it. Forget any preconceptions about juggling and concentrate, as this is all about timing. Take two balls, one in each hand. Starting again from your weak hand, throw as you have learned ("Throw"). As this ball peaks, throw the second ball from your strong hand toward your weak hand ("Throw"). At this stage, do not worry about catching either ball at first: just ensure that the timing of each throw is consistent. Once you have this timing in mind, catch the balls as they fall – saying "Catch" as you do so. At this point, you should be saying "Throw; throw – catch; catch."

6 Again, once you are comfortable with this step, reverse it and start with your stronger hand, throwing toward your weaker one.

The Three-ball Cascade (or, How to Juggle)

Don't

7 Beware at this stage of reverting to Two-ball Shuffle, where you throw from one hand to the other and then shuffle the second ball to your first hand. While there is a place for this in juggling, it is not here. Each hand should cleanly throw a mirror image of the other.

8 Now you are very nearly there, just a couple of very simple steps to go. The first of these is to take two balls in your weak hand and one in your strong. Repeat steps 6 and 7, getting used to having an extra ball in your weak hand.

9 And do the same with your strong hand.

10
So here we are, back where we started: two balls in your weak hand and one on your strong. Repeat the last exercise, but as the second ball peaks, throw the third ball from your weak hand – anywhere you like.

11
By this time, the second ball will probably have hit the floor, so don't worry about catching it – say, "Throw; throw; (catch) THROW."

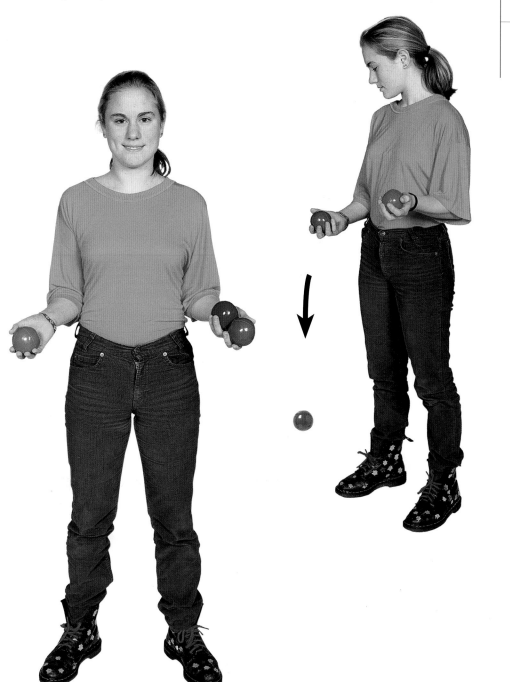

Tip

● Many people find it very difficult to let go of the third ball – it seems to be stuck to your hand. This is why at this stage we recommend throwing the third ball anywhere you like, just to get used to the feeling of letting it go.

The Three-ball Cascade (or, How to Juggle)

12 Now we want to continue this step, but catching all the balls. Aim to throw the third ball in the same way as the others, so that you end up with two balls in your strong hand and one in your weak. This is the penultimate step, so practice it well until you are confidently throwing and catching on a consistent basis.

13 The last stage is just a continuation of this movement. As the third ball peaks, throw the ball in your strong hand back toward your weak hand and as the third peaks, throw the one in your weak hand back to your strong — maintain this as long as you can, because at this stage, you are JUGGLING!

The Three-ball Cascade is truly rewarding. Once you have achieved the basic movement you will set yourself greater goals in terms of how many times you can juggle without dropping, or how high you can throw and still juggle, or even how low you can throw. But after a while, what then? Here are a few simple tricks that you can practice while you are still mastering the basics.

Over the Top

Once you have practiced the single over-the-top lob, try one with the other hand until you are proficient with either hand.

1 This is most people's very first trick. Rather than an inward throw, the hand moves outside and lobs the ball over the top of the box.

2 You will have to move your catching hand outside its normal position in order to achieve a fluid movement.

Tip

● You will find that, as the ball going over the top has to travel a greater distance than normal, you will have plenty of time on your hands to throw the next two balls. If you throw them in your normal time, you will find that one comes down at the same time as the over-the-top ball, so do not be in a hurry to throw them – or throw them a little higher than normal, being careful not to let them collide with the over-the-top.

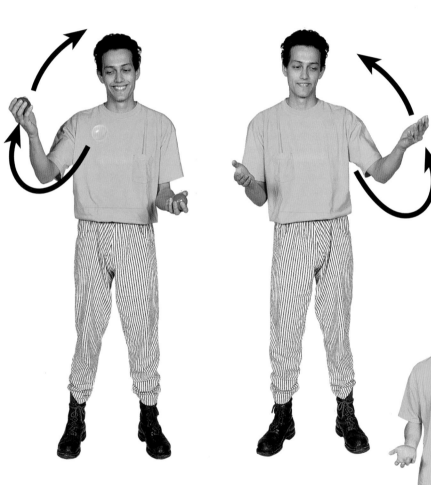

Reverse Cascade

This is a progression from Over the Top, where every single throw is an "over-the-top." Start with a normal cascade, and throw a single over-the-top throw. Then try two in a row, one with each hand. Finally move to a continuous pattern, which is very attractive, with the balls appearing to go up the outside and come down the middle, rather than the normal cascade pattern.

Columns

Many juggling patterns require ball movements other than the one we have learned so far. The first of these is for two balls to be juggled in one hand, either in a circular motion, or, as here, with the two balls moving up and down in a parallel motion – a column. A third ball may be thrown in synchronization with the outer ball.

1 Taking two balls in one hand, one in the other, throw the first ball vertically upward.

2 Moving your hand smartly outward, as the first ball peaks, throw the second and third balls vertically upward, parallel with the first. Moving your hand back inward, catch the first ball and send it up again and continue the movement.

● **The timing here is unusual, as you will find you have two balls in two hands at the same time. In order to buy extra time in the cascade, throw the central ball a little higher than normal before launching the other two balls back into the pattern.**

3

To return to the cascade pattern from columns, on catching the central ball, project it back into a cascade pattern instead of its vertical motion. As the two outer balls fall to hand, project one then the other into the cascade and continue.

This basic column pattern leads to a very simple trick – the Dummy Elevator – in which one hand juggles two balls in a column, as explained, and the other hand – without letting go of its ball – moves up and down in synchronization with the outside ball of the column pair, making the pattern look like three elevators going up and down. It is known as the Dummy Elevator because the third ball is not thrown, but carried up and down. While this concept of dummying is covered in much greater detail in Chapter 4, you may like to try it out here. (We meet the Dummy Elevator again in Chapter 4.)

Also try the circular pattern as an alternative. This will not only break up your practice and give you more confidence in your juggling, but has the additional benefit that it is the basic move required to juggle four balls (see Chapter 3). Take two balls and throw the first in a cascade-like move, but throwing it outward from your body. As it peaks, the second ball follows it in an identical trajectory. Swiftly move your hand outward to catch the first ball and propel it back into the air, following the second ball. This movement can also be made starting from the outside and moving inward toward the body.

Rainbow Cross

This is a very attractive trick and, when done well – once or twice in the middle of a Three-ball Cascade routine – it is very impressive. In order to be able to do the Rainbow Cross, you must be proficient with both the Three-ball Cascade and Columns.

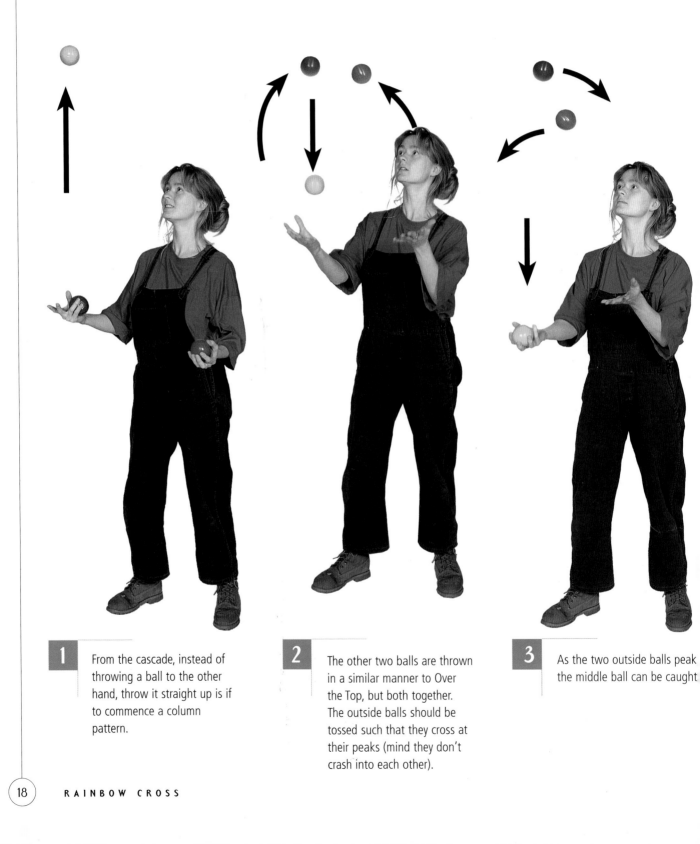

1 From the cascade, instead of throwing a ball to the other hand, throw it straight up is if to commence a column pattern.

2 The other two balls are thrown in a similar manner to Over the Top, but both together. The outside balls should be tossed such that they cross at their peaks (mind they don't crash into each other).

3 As the two outside balls peak the middle ball can be caught

4 The middle ball is then tossed again vertically and the two outside balls caught.

5 The exercise may then either be repeated, or the middle ball thrown to resume the cascade, with the two outside balls following on. Bear in mind that as you catch the two outside balls, you will have them both in your hands at the same time, so they then rejoin the cascade one at a time. Do not rush this step — take your time.

Three-ball Shower

We said earlier in the chapter that the Two-ball Shuffle had no place there, but would be used elsewhere. The shower in all its forms is essentially the same pattern: that is, the balls follow each other in the same movement.

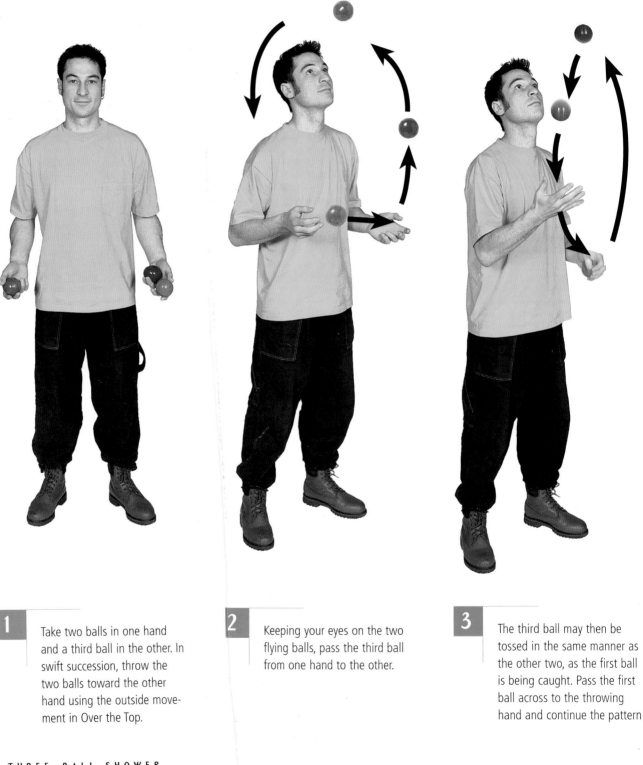

1 Take two balls in one hand and a third ball in the other. In swift succession, throw the two balls toward the other hand using the outside movement in Over the Top.

2 Keeping your eyes on the two flying balls, pass the third ball from one hand to the other.

3 The third ball may then be tossed in the same manner as the other two, as the first ball is being caught. Pass the first ball across to the throwing hand and continue the pattern

Stance and Tips

These tips will help you develop a good juggling method and assist in future development:

Tip

● As your method improves, lower the top of the box until it is just above eye-level. This is the ideal position for advanced juggling and trickery.

Hold your hands in a comfortable attitude. Throw consistently, so that the ball drops into your hand with the minimum of hand movement.

Continue to imagine the box in front of you as you juggle and aim to make the basic movements impact the box where appropriate – inside the box for a cascade, outside for Over the Top, and so on.

Stance and Tips

You should always be looking directly in front of you, catching the peak of throws with your peripheral vision. Remember that the best clue to where the ball will drop is where it peaks

In the beginning, always start with your weak hand. Always start with the hand with the most balls in.

So now you can juggle. It is pretty certain that you will have an enormous amount of fun with your new-found ability. It is also pretty certain that, in a while – be that a couple of weeks, a couple of months, or a couple of years – you will think: What next? What can I do now, that will give me as much a personal challenge and as much personal gratification as juggling has to date? Well look no further, as we intend to demonstrate a number of different pathways which will fully answer this question for you. As we said in the introduction, many people look to different equipment to fulfill their ambition. So on to Clubs …

CHAPTER 2

Clubs

So you can juggle (if not, we recommend you go back to Chapter 1 as clubs are not the ideal item for a complete beginner). You have completely mastered three balls and are looking for a new challenge? Great, because clubs are an ideal next step, a little more challenging and quite a lot more impressive.

A club is not quite as simple an object as it first appears. It is – or at least it should be – a well-constructed and weighted object, designed to spin at a specific rate. Other than personal preference, there is a reason behind the different spin rates. A beginner needs to have a club that spins quite quickly, whereas a more advanced juggler requires a slower spin – which he or she can then adjust with the requisite wrist action.

1 There are three distinct parts to the club – the body, or "bulb," the handle, and the knob. In the cheapest clubs, which are one-piece injection-molded items, all these parts are made of the same material and molded in the same process. More expensive clubs are two-piece and made normally with an injection-molded body and wooden handle.

We recommend that you start with a quality, weighted one-piece club (actually, we recommend you start with three of them: juggling with one club is not at all impressive).

The basic Three-club Cascade uses the same pattern as we used for balls and should take only a short while to master – say a long weekend. The moment when it all fits into place is as fulfilling as was the original ball cascade, but clubs are far more mesmeric, both to the participant and to their audience – it is the closest thing to licensed showing off. As very few people believe that it is within their grasp, it also provides a mental and physical challenge, giving a real boost to self-confidence once mastered. **2**

Clubs

3 The first step is to get a feel of the clubs and find a suitable holding position or grip. The club should be held just under the center line, which will give you maximum control for a nice, gentle spin.

Tips

● Warm up your shoulder muscles before you start. Club juggling is a strenuous exercise and involves extensive use of the arm, shoulder, and neck muscles.

● If your clubs do not have a well-defined center-line, then stick some colored tape where it is. This will help you grip consistently in the correct place on the club.

Don't

4 Don't hold the club too far down the handle. This is a common mistake and results in a lack of control – the club ends up far too high, or is thrown forward.

5 Taking one club, gently toss it from hand to hand. The action is similar to tossing a ball, although you will notice that the action needs to be wider than with balls because of the spin of the club. This picture shows the exaggerated arm action necessary.

6 The club should peak at about shoulder height and should spin one complete time, allowing the handle to fall comfortably into the other hand. Try not to flick the club, but allow it to spin naturally.

Tip

● Don't try to learn clubs in a restricted space. Leave yourself plenty of room – a backyard is ideal. Don't juggle near windows, small children, china, glass, any breakables or ice sculptures!

Clubs

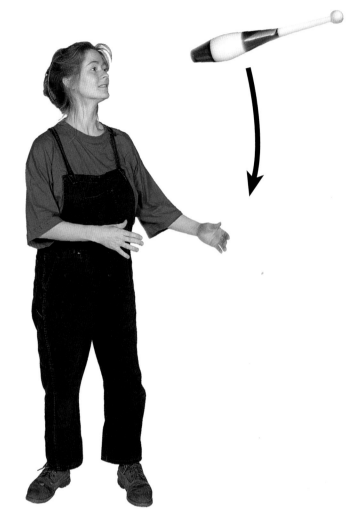

7 Repeat with the other hand and alternate, throwing from either hand until you feel relaxed and confident with both. As with juggling balls, say "Throw" each time you let go. This will help with the timing.

8 The trajectory of a club is slightly higher and wider than that of a ball, so relax your shoulders and drop your arms a little lower than you would with balls.

Tip

● When catching the club, aim for the same position you held before you released it. As with all juggling, the accuracy of the throw determines how easy is the catch. Practice the throw until you are comfortable it is accurate and consistent.

Don't

9 Don't grab or reach for the club, but let your throw result in its falling into your hand. Clubs are much more likely to collide in mid-flight than balls, so you have to be much more accurate with the throw – hence the need for a wider and higher pattern.

10 Before you pick up a second club, pick up a ball in your strong hand. Now toss the club from your weak hand to your strong hand and the ball from your strong hand to your weak. Once you are happy with this, alternate. This will allow you to get used to the timing and release of your second object before introducing the complex motion of a club into the equation

Clubs

11 Now, forget the ball and pick up the second club. Repeat the previous exercise with the clubs – again, saying "Throw" each time you release a club.

12 Repeat the same exercise, starting with your alternate hand. If you find the club is being thrown away from you, or too close to your head, recheck your hold and grip. It is at this stage that habits are formed, so try to practice the correct hold until it feels absolutely natural.

13 In addition to the grip, check your swing. You should be relaxed and swinging freely from your elbow (compare this with the wrist actions necessary for juggling balls). If catching the club is awkward try not to worry as this will come with practice and a good, consistent throw.

14 Back to the ball. Take a club in each hand and add the ball to your weak hand. Try the basic cascade pattern, starting with the clubs and finishing with the ball. Wait for each object to peak before releasing the next. Relax and take it slowly. At this stage, it is probably unnecessary to remind you that clubs are generally twice the weight of balls and quite a bit harder – you have found this out for yourself.

15 Repeat this exercise starting from the alternate hand. Try to get used to the feeling of the additional weight of the clubs and practice until you feel confident. Repeat this exercise starting from the alternate hand. Try to get used to the feeling of the additional weight of the clubs and practice until you feel confident.

Clubs

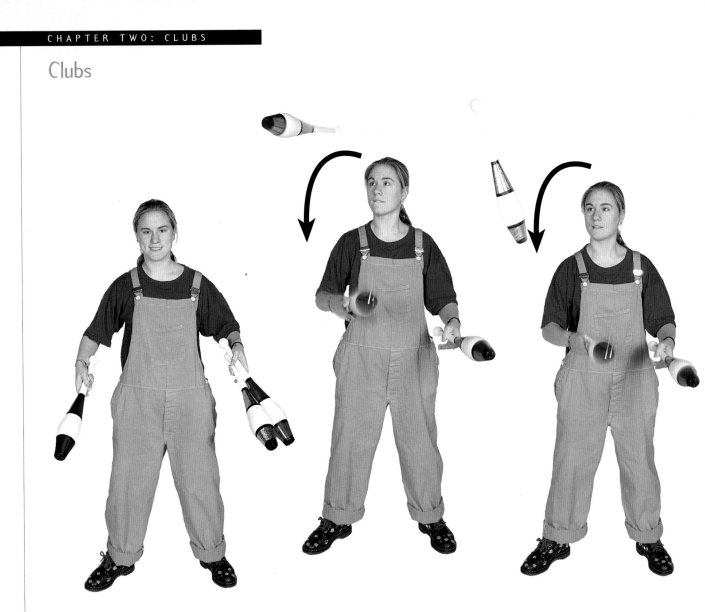

16 So let's lose the ball for good. To be able to juggle three clubs requires that you can hold two in one hand to start with. Hold the clubs so that the knob of the inner club is under the knob of the outer. Weigh up the extra weight of the third club. This position may seem a little uncomfortable at first, so adjust it to suit your hand and grip.

17 The club you are going to release first is the inner of the two. Practice releasing the first club and catching it in the other hand. The weight of two clubs in one hand is discon-certing and worth a little practice in order to achieve a consistent toss. Your fingers can be used on the underside of the club to gain additional leverage if required.

18 The importance of achieving a consistent toss cannot be overemphasized. Aim for the peak of each toss to be just above shoulder height, and in line with the shoulder itself. This will ensure that the club falls naturally to hand.

Key Stage

19 With two clubs in the starting hand and one in the other, launch the first club. As it peaks, launch the second club.

20 Catch the first club and as the second club peaks, launch the third. Try to maintain this pattern for, say, three iterations. Then stop. Catching two clubs in one hand is as awkward as starting with two, but persevere – having managed two or three complete cascade movements, you will be feeling very cocky anyway, so the feeling will soon pass. And who cares if at this stage you drop a club to finish the movement? If you have the problem consistently, then just don't stop!

From this point on, it is just practice. Challenge yourself to improve your technique, increasing the number of cascade recitals completed before dropping. Above all, practice a consistent toss, making sure the height and speed are aimed at making the catch as easy as possible. And then congratulate yourself on your achievement!

Club Control: Spins and Height

So far we have covered the basic Three-club Cascade. This will take some time to really feel natural, but once it begins to do so, you will want to add yet more to the repertoire. Clubs are a great deal more versatile than balls in this respect. After all, if you spin a ball during a toss, not only does it have almost no effect on its flight characteristics, but neither does it have any effect on your audience. Not so with clubs. Spinning a club an extra time on its own is hugely impressive and, built into a routine with other tricks, it will have your audience gasping — and leave a huge grin on your own face!

This section deals with the basic club skills and techniques which will improve your control over all aspects of your juggling and open a number of doors to more advanced tricks.

1 Take one club and hold as normal. Check your grip to ensure you have not got into a bad habit.

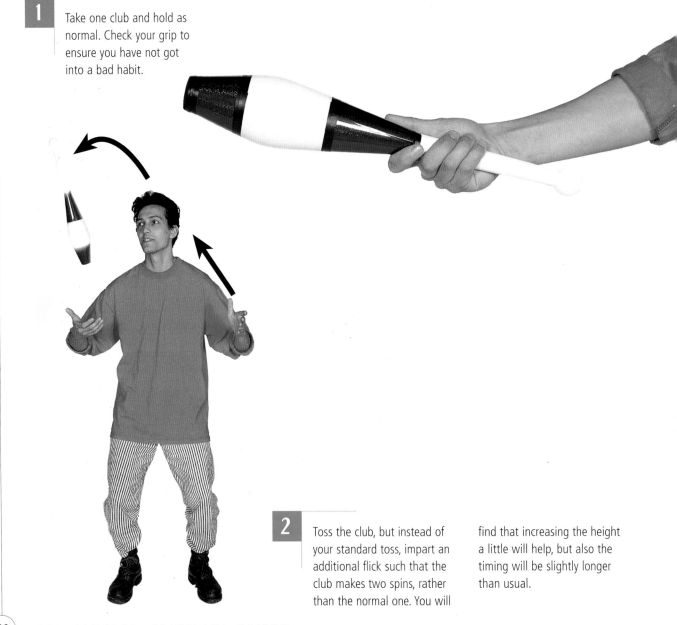

2 Toss the club, but instead of your standard toss, impart an additional flick such that the club makes two spins, rather than the normal one. You will find that increasing the height a little will help, but also the timing will be slightly longer than usual.

Spinning is the most basic advanced technique in club juggling, but it will improve your control immeasurably and is just soooooo impressive. Once the basic technique is mastered, the route to further improvement is just practice, practice, and more practice.

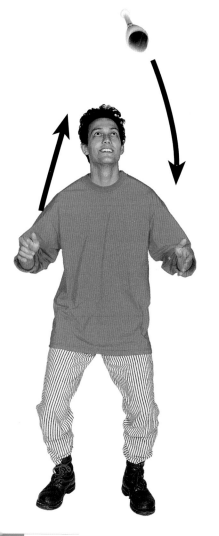

3 Practice with your alternate hand until you feel comfortable with either. Then with three clubs, practice the cascade, introducing an occasional double spin in the middle of a cascade until you can do two or three consistently. Note that the pattern will be considerably slower than normal, so try not to rush.

4 The third element of basic club control is the swing and the timing of the release. During basic cascade practice, alter your swing or the timing of the release and note the effect. See how high you can toss a club and maintain a single spin.

Tips

● **Triple spins require the same technique, with more wrist action, greater height, and more time.**

● **Height control is as important in ensuring that your multispins are successful as is the wrist action, which determines the speed of spin. Practice different heights and spin speeds, the higher the throw, the less spin speed is required to achieve the requisite number of spins.**

● **You will find that high spin speeds are more visually exciting, but of course they require a good deal more practice. Start with good height and reduce over time and practice.**

● **The final point to make here on height control is that it is an invaluable method of "buying" additional time when attempting the more ambitious maneuvers – or when attempting to correct a situation rapidly getting out of hand. Practice on height techniques will repay a thousandfold in the future.**

Club Control: Spins & Height

5 Alternatively, see how low you can toss a club. By using a greater arm movement and less of a wrist action, you will find that you can slow the clubs down so much they seem to float through the air. Again, as well as being enormously impressive, the additional time it gives you as a performer allows adjustment in stance or grip if things are getting a little pear-shaped.

Tip

● **Juggling does not have to be undertaken at full speed. In fact, the slower it is, the more graceful and controlled it looks.**

Spinning also lends itself to an alternative finish to the basic cascade. Throw a double or a triple spin quite high and, during the extra time it is in the air, transfer both the remaining clubs to one hand and catch the last club in your free hand. This is more impressive than the standard finish, especially if you are still having problems catching two clubs in one hand.

So, the basic cascade is mastered and club control is perfect. Let's have a look at some basic tricks which utilize and improve on the skills we have just learned.

Under the Leg

Although this is a very flashy trick, it is also one of the easiest. In fact the most difficult part of this trick is to determine which leg you are steadier on when the other is up in the air.

Tip

● In approaching this trick, you may find it easier if you practice a slow spin with one club in the middle of a cascade pattern, aiming for the under-the-leg to be the move straight after – the extra split second of the slow spin will come in handy in perfecting the timing of this trick.

1 The leg movement is simply to lift your leg as high as is comfortable, keeping the knee bent so that the club can be passed underneath your thigh. Try this movement with a single club at first to see the effect on timing. You may find it easier to hold the club further toward the knob than is normal. This will help with the throw and slow down the club.

2 In all other respects the throw is standard, so the catch should be standard too. When you feel comfortable with the movement, introduce it in the middle of a cascade pattern. You will find the additional body movements a lot to think about at first, but they will quickly fall into place.

As previously, when you are happy with your strong leg, try alternating with the other leg. Eventually, you should be able to do an under-the-leg throw with every other club under alternate legs. While this looks rather like a really drunk sailor's hornpipe, it will improve your skills and control and leave you very confident with moving while juggling.

Two In One hand

There are a number of tricks that involve being able to juggle two clubs in one hand. It is also quite a useful skill to have which will enable you to continue your performance without pause, should something drastic happen – such as, you've dropped something.

1 As with balls, there are two basic patterns for two-in-one-hand juggling. The first and probably easier of the two is a column pattern, with each of the clubs moving parallel to the other. You will find it much easier to use double spins as the additional time obtained will be appreciated. Practice this with each hand.

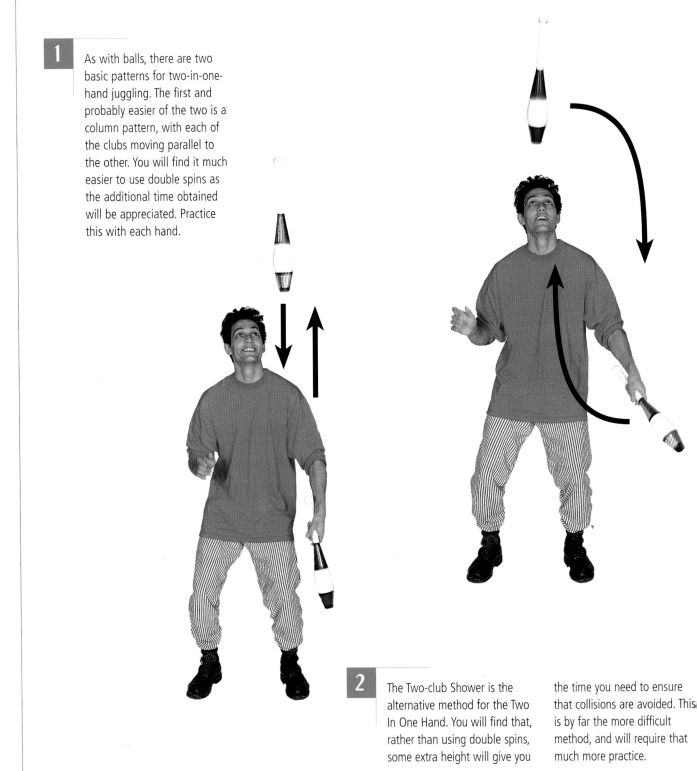

2 The Two-club Shower is the alternative method for the Two In One Hand. You will find that, rather than using double spins, some extra height will give you the time you need to ensure that collisions are avoided. This is by far the more difficult method, and will require that much more practice.

Columns and One-up, Two-up

Leading on naturally from the Two In One Hand, this is an impressive trick with a highly unimpressive and thoroughly unoriginal name. We covered this trick with balls in Chapter 1, but, as with many of these tricks, doing exactly the same movements with clubs rather than balls is vastly more entertaining.

1 Start with a club in each hand and practice throwing each vertically at the same time, ensuring that sufficient height for a double spin is achieved. When the clubs peak, clap your hands twice. This illustrates that you have ample time for the third club. Now with three clubs, commence a cascade pattern, then toss one club straight up the middle with a double spin.

2 Catching the other two clubs, throw them each up the outside, as in the earlier exercise. You will note that the continuance of this pattern is effectively a Two In One Hand with one hand, while the other is just tossing a single club vertically in time with the outside club of the other hand.

3 To make this trick really impressive, alternate catching and throwing the middle club with each hand. This can be even further improved by moving your body left and right, rather than your hands — perhaps even jumping left and right while the clubs appear stationary in the air. To move back from this pattern to the cascade, the trajectory of the middle club needs to be altered first, as with balls.

The Helicopter

This is a great-looking trick which looks exactly as its name suggests. With fire clubs it is completely stunning, although as it is also a trick which is amazingly prone to going wrong, you are well advised to:

- Practice it first with standard clubs
- Wear an asbestos cap when you first try it with fire clubs.

1 Start with Two In One Hand. Although this trick can be done using columns, it is most impressive when using the shower pattern. The third club should be held in your other hand – adjust your normal grip so that you are holding it close to the knob, but not so close that it will fly out of your hand as you swing it.

2 The third club needs to be swung over your head in a horizontal pattern. The timing of this is crucial as it should pass through the trajectory of the other two clubs at the point where they are somewhere else. Failure of this timing is evidenced by a very satisfying "thwacking" sound and a highly dissatisfactory sight of a club speeding off in another direction completely.

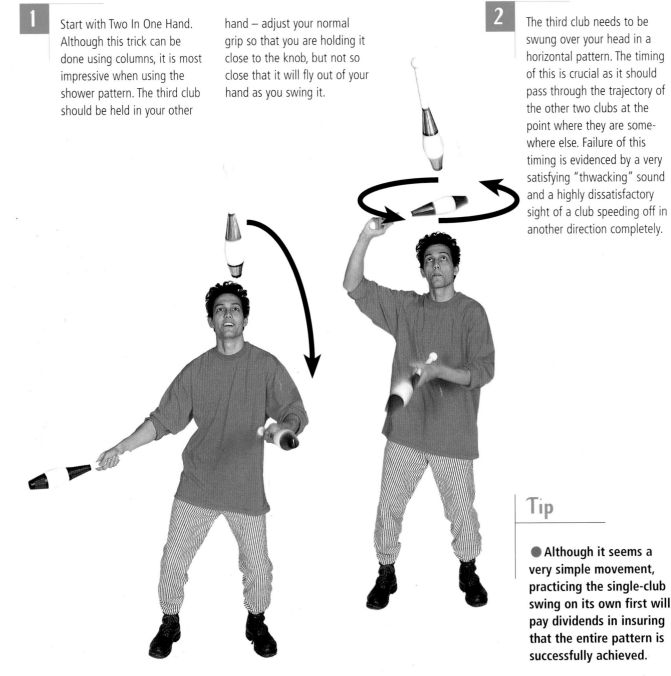

Tip

● **Although it seems a very simple movement, practicing the single-club swing on its own first will pay dividends in insuring that the entire pattern is successfully achieved.**

As the name suggests, the sight of a successful Helicopter is a main rotor going round and round horizontally, missing the tail rotor, as that goes round and round in the vertical plane. Try to move into and out of this pattern from a standard cascade in order to practice the timing of different patterns. Happy flying!

The Club Kick-up

If you have ever watched a juggling performance, you will have seen this trick – and you will want to master it yourself. The ability to kick up a club while juggling two or more others is to be able to really impress – and you can even make it look as if you dropped that club on purpose, just to be able to show off the kick-up. Alternatively, it is a very special way to "kick-start" a routine.

Tips

● Be warned, leather shoes and kick-ups do not go well together. They do not really have the necessary flex in them for this trick. Also beware of slippery floors.

● To incorporate this into a pattern where you are already juggling, two clubs should be being looked after by a Two In One Hand routine. The third club is kicked up from the floor as one of the clubs in the column pattern is launched into a cascade. The third club is collected by the hand on the same side and projected into the cascade pattern, which may then be continued.

1 The club should be placed such that the body lies outside the foot with the handle caught between your foot and shin. Lift your toes to give extra grip.

2 Step forward with the other foot, or just lift the "kicking" foot, raising the knee, and kick up the club with your heel. The club will be tossed up in a motion not dissimilar to a normal one. Note that you will catch the club in the hand on the same side as the foot that kicked it up – do not attempt to kick hard enough to toss across your body, or you will become a regular visitor to your local surgical support stockist.

The kick-up movement will take a lot of practice to perfect prior to incorporating it into your routine – and it is worth that practice. Attempts to bring it into your juggling before you are completely at ease with it may result in disaster as you try to correct the balance problems associated with juggling with one foot in the air.

Advanced Club Tricks

This brings us to the end of the basic club section. You have learned the basic Three-club Cascade and a number of solid and impressive-looking tricks. Practice all these diligently and they will not only give you incredible satisfaction, the adoration of your chosen audience, and an ego the size of an ostrich egg, but they will also be the building blocks of good club control and technique. Learned well, they will provide a solid basis for some advanced trickery.

What next on the juggling pathway? To the committed club juggler, more advanced tricks. So we cannot really finish this section without a few extra advanced tricks for our new-found friends.

The Three-club Flash

This is not only a good-looking trick, but it has a couple of additional uses. The first of them is that it is a great exercise before progressing to the amazing and difficult Five-club Cascade (covered in Chapter 4). The other is that it permits an additional split-second gap during which you can employ some "business" (see the performance section in Chapter 8) such as hand claps or a pirouette. The flash may be considered a timing change as opposed to a pattern in itself, so does not take long to master.

 First, during a standard cascade pattern, alter the height of your throws to a little higher than normal – of course, this will require slight alterations to both swing and release timing. If you have a problem with this, then revise the Club Control section. One club should practice a double spin, peaking at a height just above your eye line.

2 When all is calm, attempt to throw two consecutive doubles at the required height and continue practicing until consistent. Note the increase in time required for the two doubles to take place and the delay in release of the third to compensate.

3 The key to the flash is for all three clubs to be tossed into double spins – but for them all to be in the air at the same time. At first, limit yourself to a clap of the hands in the time they are all airborne.

4 Once you can clap twice, you've reached perfection in the flash and a pirouette can be achieved in the same time. This can be done by speeding up the timing of the release so that you are no longer waiting for the peak to be reached by the previous club before releasing the next.

Tomahawks

The Tomahawk is very much an advanced throw, as it requires a completely new action. It is this action, however, that makes it such an attractive throw, especially when built into a routine. As its name suggests, its action is rather like the trajectory of an American Indian weapon, as it heads toward an unsuspecting (or very frightened) cowboy.

1 The action required is startlingly similar to an overhead tennis serve. Take a single club and practice the action, launching it over your head to catch in the other hand. The spin required on the club is counter to the action we have used to date and will require the use of your thumb as well as your wrist to "push" the club up and over the top of your head. Do not try too hard, as, unlike the case of the Indian, the requirement here is not to bury the implement in an enemy's head, but to catch it gently in your other hand.

2 The major difficulty with this throw is in the timing and the placement of your hands. To get the Tomahawk action built into a regular pattern, the club needs to be placed in position. This is achieved using a two-stage process. From a standard cascade pattern, first allow the trajectory of the desired club to veer from its standard path so that it is heading behind your head; then, secondly, it needs to be caught just after it has peaked, rather than waiting for it to fall (behind your back in this trajectory).

4 The double Tomahawk is achieved using additional wrist/thumb action to achieve a double spin. As with other doubles, extra height will be required and the timing adjusted to fit.

Tip

● **Try to slow down the action of the Tomahawk by using your thumb to control the club into a more vertical motion. The time this takes will also help to sort out the odd timing of the throw within a standard cascade.**

3 Now, having caught the club early, you must now allow for this in the timing of your throw, so don't be in too much of a hurry to launch the Tomahawk throw. Pause a heartbeat, then toss it forward. The club's trajectory now will be heading well forward, so ignore all previous advice and reach out to snatch it from the air. The counterpoint in this timing is part of the attraction of the action.

5 Once you have practiced sufficiently with each hand in turn, try a continuous Tomahawk from one hand or the other. Attractive enough in itself, this may be further enhanced by alternating single and double spins.

Balancing

Balancing objects seems to be a common passion of jugglers, and is addictive, if at least not fattening. Almost any object that can be juggled is fair game for a further stint as a balanced object, and (almost) literally any part of the body is fair game to be balanced upon. (Please note here that if you want to use the sink-plungers we suggest in a later chapter, only one end of the plunger should be used!) In addition to balancing, jugglers are extremely fond of using as much of their bodies as possible to incorporate into their routines. "If you can't balance on it, throw something over or under it" is the basic maxim.

Balancing is not difficult, but will enhance a fairly ordinary juggling routine due to the counterpoint of its timing and the additional degree of difficulty it places on a seemingly "easy" juggling pattern. Clubs are ideal to start with – you have them to hand anyway – as their weight and internal balance are well known to you.

1 The hand balance is the easiest place to start. Place the club in the center of your palm (bulb uppermost, or it is not hugely impressive!), with your hand flat and outstretched. Making sure that it is perfectly vertical, let go of the club. Focus your eyes on the top of the club and anticipate its toppling action by moving your hand in the same direction. Do not move any other part of your body, and use very small movements, each one of which will normally require an immediate counteraction (hopefully smaller than the first). Practice this until you can keep the club balanced consistently for more than 20 seconds.

2 Probably the most common balance used in juggling is the chin balance. Although it helps to have a "granite jaw" like those of the men in the razor ads, skill is actually the more important attribute here, and it is the conjunction of eye contact and the ability to move the part of the body on which you are balancing that enables this skill (you may also find it useful to suspend all belief in gravity and suchlike). Place a club on the chin and again focus on the top of the club, trying to ensure it is perfectly vertical.

3 Now make like a seal. The neck action here is not one the body is used to and the problem is exacerbated with the head thrown back at an awkward angle. Nevertheless, the action required is identical to that practiced with the hand, anticipating any fall of the club head with a move in the same direction. Do not "overcontrol" as this will result in the correcting movements getting bigger and bigger.

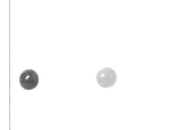

Experiment for yourself using common – non-juggling – items. Umbrellas, broomsticks, and bottles are all fair game, but please practice with something not too heavy and completely unbreakable first. It is not so impressive to have a black eye.

4 Another favorite position is the bridge of the nose. Mistakenly, most people believe that a place to "cradle" the balancing object is needed and the dip formed between your forehead and nose seems ideal for the job. In actual fact, as anyone who has ever "hung" a spoon on their nose will tell you, surface friction is by far the most important attribute. The technique for balancing is identical to a chin balance.

Tips

● **Larger and heavier objects are, to a degree, easier to balance with as they are less susceptible to wind and movement – try an umbrella for example.**

● **Relax. If you tense up, not only will you find this reflects in the club's movements, but you will also end up with a very stiff neck. Plant your feet in a comfortable stance and keep them still while your neck makes most of the movements.**

● **This pattern may be exercised in a continuous movement with one hand. This is made much easier by placing the catching hand up high to catch the incoming club early and positioning it on the chin in one quick movement. Alternatives to the chin such as the knee or foot – can be used to good effect for the same trick.**

5 Once you have mastered a couple of basic balances, it is time to incorporate them into your routine. One of the more effective tricks is to utilize chin-balancing within a standard cascade pattern. Rather than letting a club fall to hand, catch it just as it peaks and immediately balance on your chin, allowing it to overbalance so that it falls into the hand it was originally intended for. Although it's not strictly a balancing action, as the movement is continuous, you will need the balancing skills already gained to achieve a perfectly timed fall in the correct direction. Practice will improve the timing of this, as the placement and fall will not be identical to the normal movement. Once you have perfected this, the movement can become more of a pause and balance, rather than a continuous one.

Back Cross

A common flash start for the ball jugglers is to launch a number of balls from behind the back, over the head. While this is impractical for club jugglers, a common move is the Back Cross, which takes one club behind the back and over the shoulder in a similar movement. Do not be put off by the awkwardness of the move – although a crash helmet may come in useful until you have the basics pinned down.

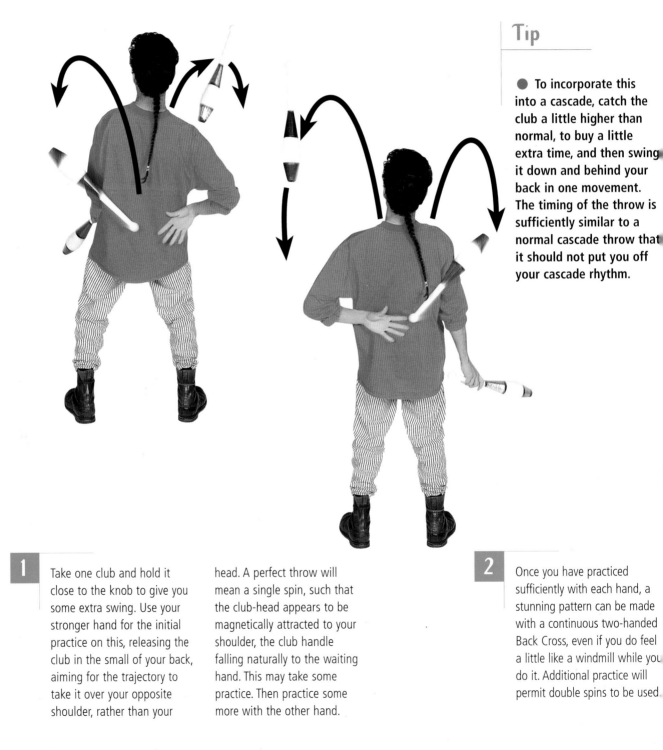

Tip

● **To incorporate this into a cascade, catch the club a little higher than normal, to buy a little extra time, and then swing it down and behind your back in one movement. The timing of the throw is sufficiently similar to a normal cascade throw that it should not put you off your cascade rhythm.**

1 Take one club and hold it close to the knob to give you some extra swing. Use your stronger hand for the initial practice on this, releasing the club in the small of your back, aiming for the trajectory to take it over your opposite shoulder, rather than your head. A perfect throw will mean a single spin, such that the club-head appears to be magnetically attracted to your shoulder, the club handle falling naturally to the waiting hand. This may take some practice. Then practice some more with the other hand.

2 Once you have practiced sufficiently with each hand, a stunning pattern can be made with a continuous two-handed Back Cross, even if you do feel a little like a windmill while you do it. Additional practice will permit double spins to be used.

Between the Legs

An alternative to an Under the Leg throw is one made between the legs. The comedy element of this appeals to most public performers, but the serious student of juggling will find this is also quite a lot more difficult than the earlier trick and will want to try it for that reason (high-minded fellow that he – or she – is!).

Tip

● As you bend back-ward, try standing on your toes, as this will help your balance.

1 The club hold is similar to that used for the Back Cross, and for similar reasons. Take one club to practice the throw and, holding close to the end, bend sideways and swing the club between your legs from behind, using your wrist to toss it up in a spin (as you stand back upright) to your waiting hand. Easy, isn't it? No, you're right, it isn't. There is little more to this trick than practice and the ability to contort your body into odd positions.

2 The timing of the catch and release is similar to the Back Cross. Within a cascade pat-tern, catch the club early to make up for the transmission time "down South" and throw at a pace to enable you to regain your normal composure before having to catch.

3 For those of you not already being measured up for your straitjacket and an extremely comfortable room, an interest-ing alternative is to reverse the throw so that it goes between your legs from the front and spins up over one hip – but beware of the follow-through on this one.

Side Spins

The Side Spin is a variation on the trajectory of a club. As such it is more a technique than a pattern in itself – as with the Flash.

1 When a club is correctly launched in a Side Spin it is very much more visual as the spin of the club describes a line parallel to the line of your body. It can be seen much more easily by your audience and, as with the standard spin, can be used in single, double, or triple spins.

2 First, you need to get used to the slightly awkward grip that's required to be used, and to adjust the release. Taking one club, hold as shown, raising your elbow and turning your wrist so that it is parallel to your chest. Launch the club in a similar trajectory to the usual throw, but use the wrist to impart a horizontal spin action. Compare this movement with a normal throw, which uses just a swinging action from the entire arm.

At first, you will probably find the club spinning far too much as the amount of spin input by the wrist has to be judged. Rather than a wild flick, the action is still a rather slow and gentle lob with the arm, combined with a small wrist action.

When you are comfortable with the action with a single club, begin a Three-club Cascade and throw in a single Side Spin. The timing of the spin is identical to the normal throw, so the action fits in very well with the cascade pattern. Try to practice with each hand.

As with standard double spins, extra time is required for the club to complete the desired path and this must be built into the timing of the overall pattern. As with other double spins, the Double Side Spin can be used to gain additional time or cover another mistake.

3 Double Side Spins are visually very attractive. Two points need to be borne in mind. First, the spin needs to be a touch faster, governed by the wrist action. And secondly, the trajectory needs to be just a little higher than normal.

Practice the throw with one club. The throwing hand needs to begin the throw quite wide from the body, and with sufficient height to clear the remaining clubs being juggled. You will find that the timing is improved by making it a double rather than a single spin. As with all other juggling tricks, practice with each hand in turn.

Finally in this section, a fantastic-looking throw – the Over the Top Side Spin. As with the ball version, the figure is achieved by tossing one club up over the pattern from one hand to the other. Its attractiveness is matched by the degree of difficulty, so do not be put off if you don't get it immediately. And remember, the tricks that conclude this chapter are among the most difficult you will come across.

But each is only one step from the previous, so any time you feel you are losing the thread, go back a stage and continue to practice before reaching forward once more. Small steps are always easier to take than big ones, but it is all too common to rush a small step because it seems so easy, and several rushed small steps make one big one too many.

The Numbers Game

It has been said that on a difficulty scale of 1 to 10 the Two-ball Shuffle hardly registers. Babies toss their rattles in a good imitation and the girls in the playground learn it while skipping at the same time. We said earlier that the Three-ball Cascade was no more difficult than tying shoelaces, and on our scale here, registers probably about 4 out of 10. Clubs are a little harder, but still happily around 6 or 7. If juggling four balls can be said to be at a difficulty level of 9, what then would five balls register? For those of you with a nervous disposition, we are going to ignore that question for the moment – as four balls is our goal. Any more can wait their turn.

It seems to be part of the human psyche that as soon as one objective is achieved, we turn to the next one with barely time to savor the full enjoyment of achievement. "I can juggle with three balls and have been doing so successfully for some minutes now. It's easy! So where is the next challenge?" In the absence of clubs, many people just grab another ball – it seems logical enough. While the theory is sound, and the method simplicity itself, we have found that, as with the Three-ball Cascade, taking the steps in small, manageable bites is the most successful route.

Four Balls

Firstly, permit us to let you into a secret of four-ball juggling. In the basic movement, unlike the Three-ball Cascade, the balls never actually cross. The art is to create the impression, without having to achieve reality.

1 Take two balls in one hand and practice throwing them in a circular motion – not the parallel motion of columns. For the purposes of this exercise, it is really immaterial which hand you start with. Try to make the throws of a consistent height. Throw the ball away from your body. Your hand should start the move just on your hip, and end about a foot further out.

2 Now try to throw in the opposite direction, inward toward your body. Here your hand will start the movement about a foot outside your hip and end just on it.

3 Review the parallel-column movement, introduced in Chapter 1. These three movements should then be practiced with your alternate hand until a consistent throw can be maintained with either.

Tip

● If you have a problem with the balls getting too close together, open a door and try the same exercise with a hand either side of it.

To complete the pattern, the throws should be alternated with either hand instead of going up and down in parallel. This completes the illusion of the balls crossing, whereas in fact their trajectories never cross.

4 Now try with both hands at the same time. Do not despair if you can do only one or two complete revolutions, as working both hands together takes some pretty amazing coordination.

Half-Shower

Now you can keep all four in the air at once, let's try a variation – the Four-ball Half-Shower. You will have realized by now that when juggling even numbers, the crossing, or cascade movement, becomes nigh impossible (the numbers literally just don't add up). There are, however, a couple of methods for a more fluid crossing pattern, this one being our particular favorite.

1 Take two balls, one in each hand. These are quite simply thrown across from one hand to another at the same time, the only difficulty being that they travel at different heights – one in an Over the Top trajectory, the other much lower, really just a little toss from one hand to the other. The coordination needed is not unlike that required for rubbing your stomach and patting your head at the same time, but it becomes easier with practice.

2 If this causes difficulty, try going back to the Three-ball Shower. Practice this, then speed it up a little. Then go back to the previous step.

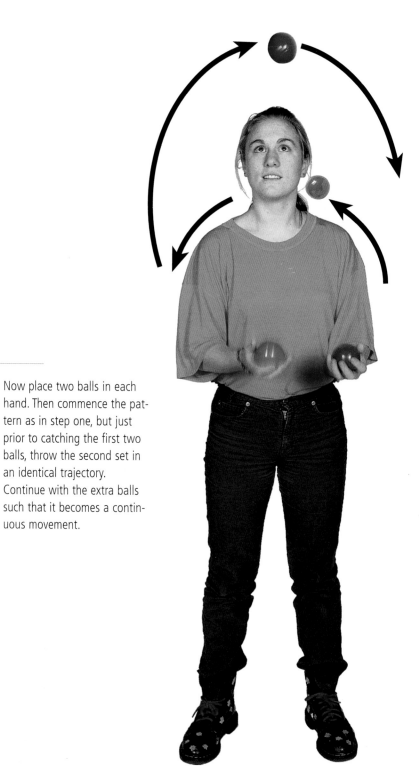

● You will find that the timing of this trick is extremely relaxed once you have got used to it, as it is just a "double" movement – two throws of two balls.

3

Now place two balls in each hand. Then commence the pattern as in step one, but just prior to catching the first two balls, throw the second set in an identical trajectory. Continue with the extra balls such that it becomes a continuous movement.

Five Balls

We said earlier that four-ball juggling scored around 9 on our difficulty scale. Not to put too fine a point on it, the scale is not really appropriate for our fifth ball, as we are talking in the early hundreds, rather than in terms of tens – it will take a great deal of commitment and practice to get to this level. But, the sense of achievement when you grasp the timings involved and begin to relax is well worth the effort – to say nothing of the show-off factor, which is just about the only thing that measures up to the difficulty factor. Juggling five balls is **impressive**.

Juggling, we maintain, is a good analogy for complex problem-solving. Don't concentrate on the big picture too early, but reduce the problem to smaller steps and solve those. As you progress, you will find more and more of the problem has been tackled and ultimately the big picture has been reduced to a series of smaller frames – all of which have been addressed and sense can be made of the whole.

In the same way as we have tackled the balls and clubs up to now, so we will tackle five balls – in a series of small, achievable steps. It is important to remember – at any point where you experience a "blockage" – to go back a step or two and practice those again until your confidence is rebuilt, before attempting the problem step again. You will find that no step we have devised is too large, given proper work on the previous one.

The basic five-ball pattern is a cascade similar to the three-ball. It is a crossing motion which follows the same principles, with the exception that, normally, there should be three balls in the air and one in each hand, at any point. Compare this with the Three-ball Cascade, which has one ball in the air and one in each hand.

Three-ball Flash

1 To start, practice the Three-ball Flash. Juggle the Three-ball Cascade, but throw the balls extra high, so that they seem to hang in the air together for a while.

2 At this point, you should have nothing in your hands, and you should aim to be able to clap your hands twice before catching the balls and sending them skywards again.

The Snake

1 The next exercise to practice is the Snake. This will get you used to releasing three balls from one hand. Begin with three balls in one hand and throw them in quick succession in a normal cascade movement to the other hand. The first ball should be being caught as the last ball leaves your hand.

2 Repeat this with the other hand until you are consistently throwing and catching. The Snake should then be maintained in a continuous pattern, such that the balls perform a "horizontal figure of eight" vertically in front of you. This is not an easy exercise, but performed correctly is an impressive pattern in its own right.

Tip

● As you throw the first ball, do not wait for it to peak as you would normally, but continue to release balls two and three as for a Three-ball Cascade, but with faster timing and throwing them higher.

Five balls

Key Stage

1 Although this is the "biggie," your mastery of the Three-ball Flash and the Snake should leave you fully confident by now. Three balls in one hand, two in the other, release the balls at the speed you used for the Three-ball Flash, but continue with the extra two. (This was the time you previously spent clapping, remember?)

2 Do not trouble yourself with catching any of them, just watch the speed at which they left your hands and the trajectory they follow. Try to ensure that they are all following the correct paths and reach a consistent height.

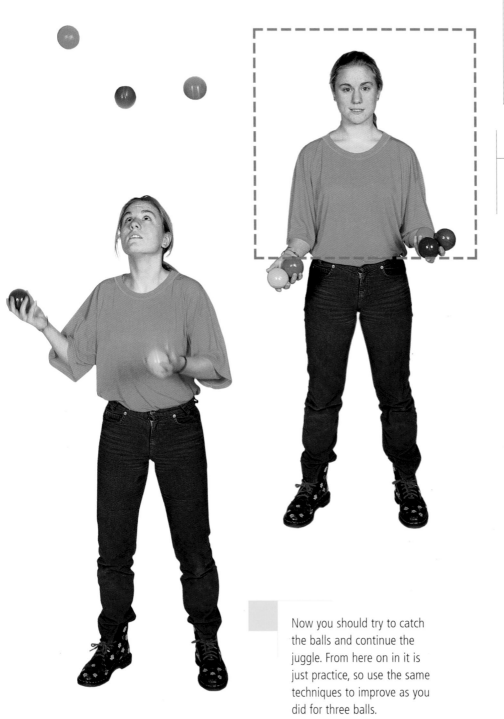

● As you throw, try to ensure you are relaxed and that each arm is releasing at the same height and strength. Little inconsistencies here show up greatly when you throw a few feet higher.

● In juggling five balls, you will also recognize that more time is required. The "box" therefore needs to be adjusted to reflect this. Throwing higher will give you more time, but will also encourage errors if your throws are inaccurate or inconsistent.

Now you should try to catch the balls and continue the juggle. From here on in it is just practice, so use the same techniques to improve as you did for three balls.

Many people will consider that successfully juggling five balls is a job well done. And we agree with them – few people reach this far, and fewer still are those that

reach it sane! So for the really mental among you, here are a couple of extra tricks for the committed five-baller.

Half-Shower

The Half-Shower for five balls is the same in theory as it is for three. Each ball from one hand only is thrown "over the top", while the other hand performs a standard cascade pattern. It is easy to run out of superlatives in dealing with five-ball tricks, but this is simply stunning to watch — and a real joy to perform.

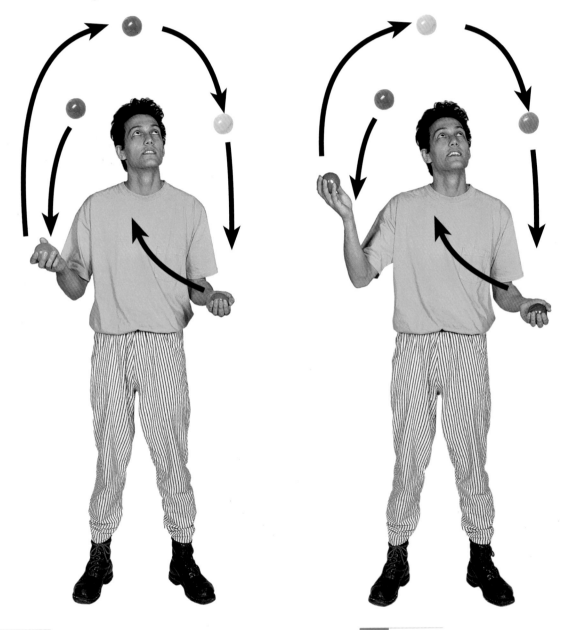

1 First, it is useful to practice a simple Over the Top from the standard cascade. As with the three-ball version, the timing alters a little, given the extra distance the ball has to travel, but this is simply absorbed. Practice with either hand.

2 Once a single Over the Top has been practiced, make it two in a row, then continue through three in a row to a continuous pattern.

Multiplex

The multiplex is so called because more than one ball is thrown in the same action. It is the basic unit used in Five-ball Columns, so will be dealt with briefly here, even though it is also a three-ball trick and is covered in more detail in that section.

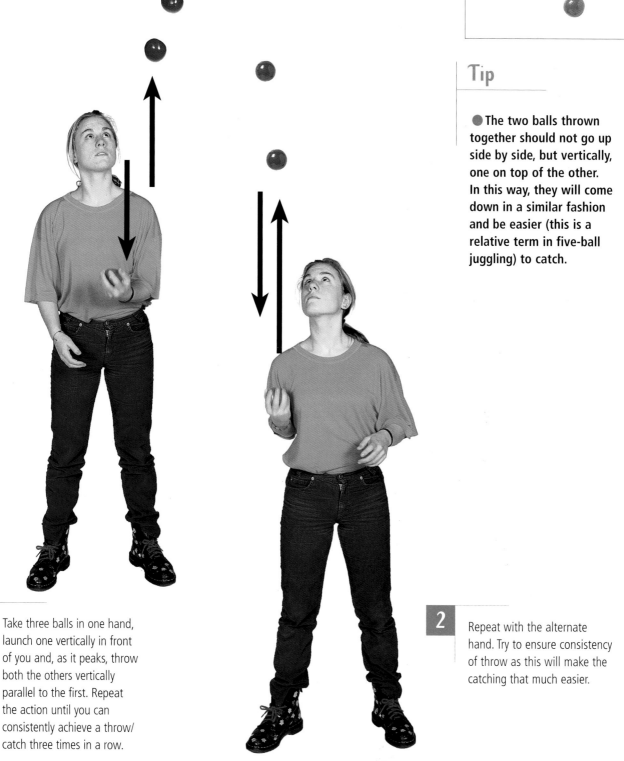

1 Take three balls in one hand, launch one vertically in front of you and, as it peaks, throw both the others vertically parallel to the first. Repeat the action until you can consistently achieve a throw/ catch three times in a row.

2 Repeat with the alternate hand. Try to ensure consistency of throw as this will make the catching that much easier.

Five-ball Columns

Columns with five-balls are achieved as follows:

1 Take three balls in one hand. This hand will perform a multi-plex, throwing a single ball vertically up the middle, while the remaining two balls move in parallel up the outside.

2 The other hand contains the remaining two balls which are thrown in tandem with the multiplexed pair. To complete the movement, alternate the hand that catches and throws the single middle ball. To return to a cascade from columns, start from the single ball, tossing it into the cascade pattern, but higher than normal to give yourself some extra time. As the multiplexed pairs fall, they can be caught and launched straight back into the original pattern (just like that).

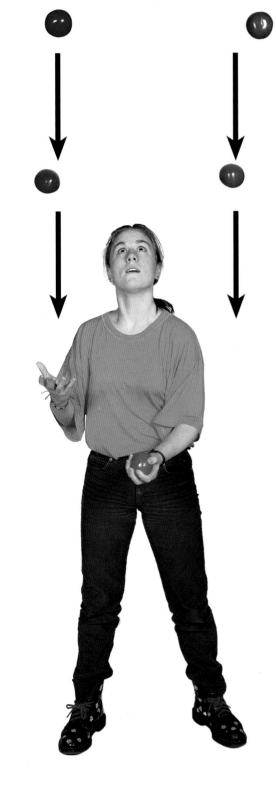

There are as many possibilities with five balls as there are with three. It just takes courage, determination, and patience. Adjustments will always be required in timing and speed, but anyone who has mastered even a basic Five-ball Cascade will be knowledgeable enough about these aspects not to have them become a problem.

More Clubs

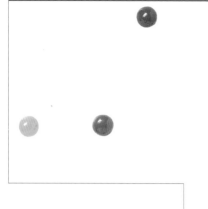

Those jugglers into the "numbers" game are not limited to ball jugglers. Club jugglers also love to move on to more and more clubs, so this section is for those of you falling into these particular depths. If you are not already the proud owner of a crash helmet, then now is a particularly apt moment to become so – as with balls, the clubs are going to be flying higher than before and whatever you might think, a disbelief in gravity is actually not going to stop them falling. If it does, please let us know first.

Four Clubs

1 As with balls, the basic pattern for four clubs is two in each hand. Start with two clubs in one hand and with the hand starting from close to the center of the body, toss the first club outward toward the shoulder. As it peaks, the second club is tossed in an identical trajectory, and the hand moved smartly outward to catch the falling first club. The hand is then moved back inward and the move repeated. You will find that this action is made easier by utilizing double spins in each throw as the extra height and spin will give you more time to place your hand in the correct position.

Tip

● Review the section on Club Control (p. 32). The slower you can make the action, the easier it is to move the hands the distance required to collect each club thrown. So throw a little higher and with double spins.

Four Clubs

2 As with four balls, it is imperative that this movement be practiced equally with each hand until you are entirely comfortable with the action.

3 Taking two clubs in each hand, launch the first club from your weaker hand, closely followed by the first club from your stronger hand. As each side peaks, the remaining club is thrown to follow.

Four-club Half-Shower

The Four-club Half Shower is a lovely-looking pattern. It is one of our favorites with balls and so too with clubs.

Tip

● **Timing is crucial to this trick. Surprisingly, the upper club does not take as huge a length of time to complete as its height will suggest.**

1 Start with a single club in each hand. You are going to throw them both at the same time to the other hand, but one has to be tossed high, with a triple spin, and the other low with a slow cascade move and a single spin. Practice this with each hand doing both moves. The trick is to try to get the timing of both these throws in synchronization.

2 Now, taking two clubs in each hand, begin the pattern, tossing the second pair in identical trajectories to the first pair, just before you catch the first pair.

Five Clubs

Juggling five clubs is more difficult than juggling five balls, even though it uses the same pattern. Having three clubs in the air at any one time in a cascading pattern is risking collision on a major scale and the avoidance of this takes much practice.

1 Start with three clubs in one hand. The hold is an extension of the two-club hold and uses each remaining club as a lever for the preceding one. As with balls, start by practicing the Three-club Flash. Use double spins on each throw and get to the position where you can clap twice during the Flash while the three clubs are in the air. As with all club work, accuracy is more important in the release, as this will ensure that the catch is as easy as possible.

2 Practice the Snake with three clubs, launching all three from one hand so that they are caught by the other hand and immediately launched to form a "horizontal figure of eight" vertically in front of you. There is really no alternative to the next step, but the expertise in the Flash and the Snake should have left you confident in your ability to handle the timing and speed necessary.

With balls, we didn't bother to catch them at first, but this is going to be painful to try with clubs. With three clubs in your weaker hand and two in the other — and with the speed and height we used in the Three-club Flash — launch the clubs from alternate hands, continuing until you have none left, then begin a catch-and-launch sequence to continue the cascade.

Practice is all it takes, plus a store of patience and the desire to achieve what few people can. If you have reached this far, then you can do it, and good luck to you.

CHAPTER 4
More Balls Than Most

Clubs? Who needs them? Gaudy bits of plastic flying everywhere and breaking things. The really serious exponent of the fine art concentrates on the pure approach, and that means "balls." And as for the number merchants, just what is so special about adding in an extra ball? No, serious juggling means not only balls, but three balls. Well, maybe that is taking things too far. But, there are an enormous number of tricks that can be performed with three balls and the level of skill and mental agility required is no less than that required for the other pathways.

Three In One Hand

The level of dexterity required for this trick is as high as the trick is impressive. It can be made even more so if some nonchalant action can be performed with the "spare" hand. As with the Two In One Hand (see p. 36) there are a number of alternatives, columns, or circular patterns going away from and into the body. Try them all, and as with every other action we have practiced up to now, make sure you are as good with each hand.

1 Hold three balls in one hand, roughly in a triangle. The one furthest from your wrist should be released first, with the hand describing the standard movement, starting from the center of the body and tossing the ball out toward the shoulder of the same hand.

2 Do not wait until the first ball peaks, but launch the second ball to follow an identical trajectory. In similar time, let the third ball follow the first two. Move your hand smartly outward, so that each of the balls falls into it in turn. Practice this move until the throws are consistent – as are the catches. Now try again, but as the first ball falls to hand, move your hand smartly back in toward the center and relaunch the ball. Move your hand back out in time to catch the second ball and continue. Now it is just practice again.

Three In One Hand

Tip

● Make sure that the tosses are sufficiently high to give you the time to move your hand back and forth. The lower the throw, the less time you will have.

3 As with the Two In One Hand, you should also practice the reverse direction, with the balls moving up the outside and back down toward the middle of your body.

4 Additional business can be conducted with the "free" hand – an effective move is simply to pocket it (the cheat's version of five-ball juggling). Those of you with alternative skills could try spinning a basketball on one finger while juggling three balls in the other hand – or even eating an apple, drinking a soda, or humming "The Star-spangled Banner."

Column Variations

Basic columns with three in one hand require the use of a technique known as "multiplexing," which is where two balls are thrown simultaneously with the same hand.

1 Start with two balls in one hand and practice throwing them both at the same time in a vertical motion. They should both rise together, not side by side, but one on top of the other, as this makes them easier to catch. Now, with three balls in one hand, toss a single ball vertically up the middle and, as it peaks, toss the remaining two vertically parallel. The continuance of this is multiplexing, or three-in-one-hand columns.

But, don't stop there. With two balls, column variations are strictly limited, but having three balls gives an extra dimension which permits many, many variations. Try one or other of the following suggestions and then come up with a few of your own.

Figure of Eight variation

This involves two balls following a standard vertical parallel pattern while the third ball intertwines through them, using a cascade pattern.

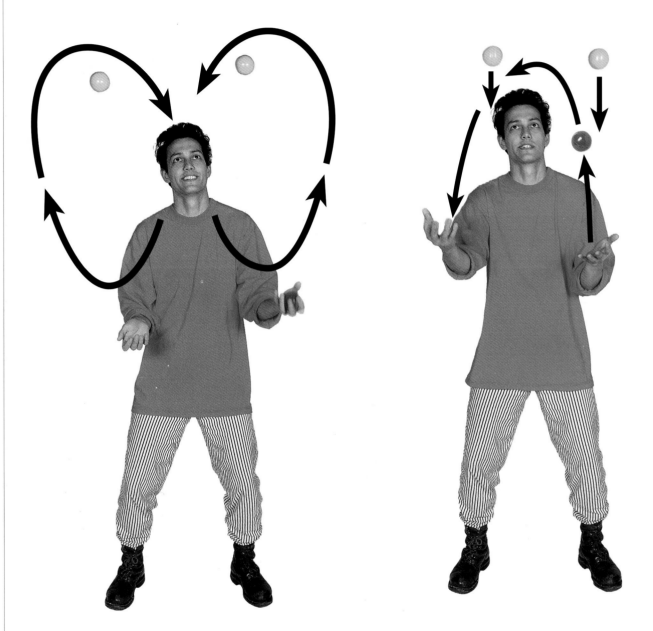

1 Start with two in one hand and one in the other, and begin the basic column pattern. Then, when the middle ball is caught, instead of sending it up the middle, throw it in a cascade movement toward the other hand.

2 As the middle balls peaks, catch the two outside balls and send them back up in their normal columns. The "middle" ball will now come down the outside of the pattern, can be caught, and sent back in a cascade movement to the other hand. As the pattern is continued, it can be seen that the "middle" ball is describing a figure of eight between the two columns.

Over the Top variation

This uses the familiar over-the-top move, but with the remaining two balls being kept in column pattern, rather than cascade, as usual.

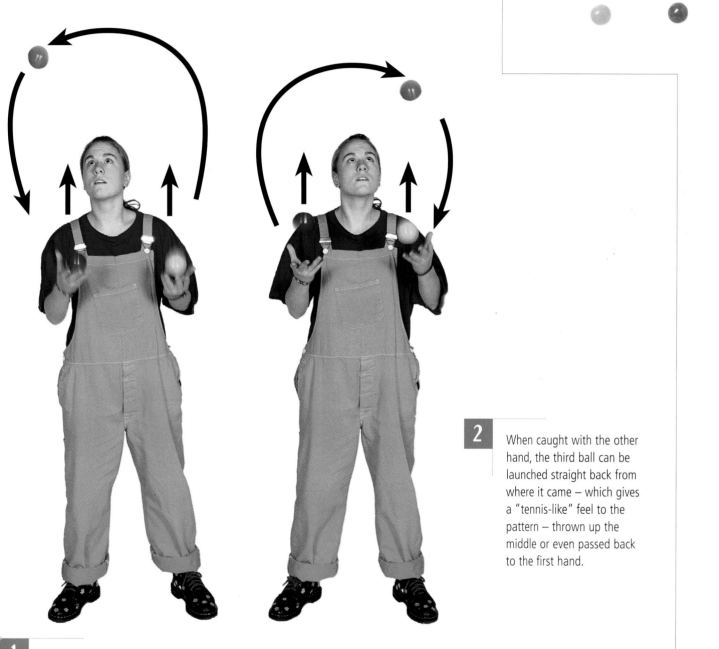

2 When caught with the other hand, the third ball can be launched straight back from where it came – which gives a "tennis-like" feel to the pattern – thrown up the middle or even passed back to the first hand.

1 Begin a standard Three-ball Column, two up the outside in parallel, one up the middle. Then, extract the middle ball and move it to the outside, launching it over the top of the other two balls' trajectories.

The joy of column variations come from the solid, dependable action of the two parallel-pathed balls being in counterpoint to the free, easy, go-anywhere nature of the third ball – rather like watching an aerial display team. Further variations can be explored using techniques learned in Under the Leg or the Back Cross (see Chapter 2).

The Box

This section would not be complete without reference to one of the most amazing of column-type variations – the Box. When this is executed correctly, the balls seem to be disappearing from one place and magically reappearing in another – while defying gravity at the same time. A visual stunner, this is not an easy trick and requires a full understanding of the very odd timing which is the key to success.

The movements of the trick are identical on each hand, so do make sure you practice consistently with each. To describe the action taking place, each hand has a ball which is thrown vertically. The third ball travels horizontally between the two hands, giving the effect of a box shape.

1 Back to basics – take just one ball. Holding your hands at the same height, throw the ball horizontally from one hand to the other. In order to get a flat trajectory, you will need to throw quite hard. Keep your hands closer together than normal.

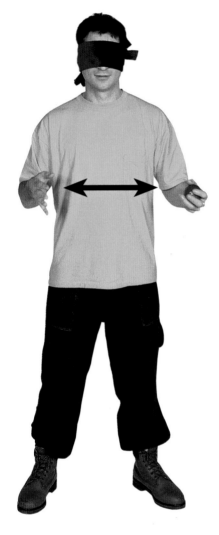

2 Continue to practice this for a short while. Now close your eyes and try again. Practice this until you can catch the ball two out of three times with your eyes closed (or blindfolded). Take two balls in one hand. Throw the first vertically and, as it reaches its peak, throw the second ball horizontally to the other hand. Catch the first ball in the original hand. Practice this movement with your alternate hand. Note the timing of the horizontal ball and adjust the vertical distance of the other ball to fit.

3 Taking three balls, begin as before. The third ball has to be thrown vertically with the alternate hand prior to catching the horizontal ball, and a heartbeat before the first ball peaks.

4 In the same timing, the horizontal ball is passed back to the original hand, which has caught and tossed the first ball prior to catching the horizontal. This pattern is then continued so that the two outside balls are moving in columns, but alternately, while the middle ball travels horizontally between the hands.

Tip

● In almost every case up until now, to verify the landing point of any ball, you have only had to concentrate on its peak. Not so with the horizontal ball here, as it shouldn't have a peak, and you need to concentrate on the peaks of the other two balls in order to assess the timing correctly. This is why it is important to be able to catch the horizontal ball without seeing it at all.

When you have mastered this trick, vary the shape of the box by altering the timing and height of the pattern, or the distance between your hands. A continuous, fluid pattern of changing shapes is really very visually exciting.

Multiplexing and Gathering

We came across multiplexing in Chapter 3 and when we spoke of Column Variations. The technique involves simultaneously throwing two or more balls with the same hand. The process of holding back one or more balls from a pattern, before projecting them back into it in conjunction with one or more other balls, is known as Gathering. Other than at a start of a pattern, the desire to use a multiplex will first require that you gather the requisite number of balls, while maintaining some sort of pattern.

1 For example, from a standard cascade pattern, you want to progress to three in one hand. In order to achieve this, one route would be to hold one ball back from the cascade pattern, and "gather" another into the same hand.

2 Launch that same ball up the middle, "gather" the third ball, and then launch the two balls up the outside before collecting the center ball again.

1

Multiplexes are used to punctuate or break up patterns. The move from one pattern to another frequently requires a change in timing which the Gather and Multiplex facilitate.

2

From a cascade pattern, gather one ball. This is done by holding onto one ball, rather than launching it into the pattern, catching and launching the second ball as normal – which keeps the pattern flowing – and catching the third ball in the same hand (you now have two balls in that hand). Now take that hand behind your back and launch both balls over your shoulder. As both balls come over your shoulder, they are to be caught one in each hand, one of which will already have a ball in it. Just before you catch the two balls, the third ball is launched into the cascade movement, with the remaining two balls following in the correct time.

Dummy Elevator and Variations

Now you may be wondering why this trick is being repeated here after being introduced in Chapter 1. The reason lies in the two words "dummy" and "variations" as this concept of faking or cheating demands to be explored further, now you have a few extra techniques to hand and an audience who require entertainment. We have seen earlier that juggling entertainment frequently employs aspects of other disciplines in order to bring it out to full effectiveness – verbal skills, balancing skills, and now cheating!

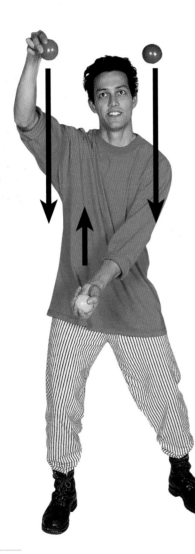

1 So review the Dummy Elevator technique under Columns in Chapter 1. The movement is simply parallel columns, but with one outside ball being lifted by hand in tandem with its opposite number, which is being thrown.

2 One variation is to use alternate hands on every "two-up" throw.

3 To do this, you will also have to alternate which hand the middle ball is being released from. This variation is definitely in the "advanced" category and will take some time to accomplish, as the switching of hands is very quick.

4 Another variation is known as the Yo-yo. Instead of dummying the outside ball, the dummy is placed about nine inches above the middle ball's trajectory. Mimicking this makes it look like the middle ball is attached to the dummy, making it look a little like that eponymous toy.

The Machine

The Machine is another advanced variation. In this, the dummy ball is replaced each iteration in a fashion that looks incredibly mechanical.

1 Begin with the Dummy Elevator, as before, but rather than just following a vertical movement with the dummy...

2 ...As you reach the peak, change direction and let the following move be horizontal, across to where the other outside ball is peaking. Then reverse direction and come back down again. Practice this until you are used to the alterations in direction.

Tips

● It helps in this to try to slow things down to start with, so throw a little higher than usual.

● The snatch action is very similar to that described overleaf, but your hand should already be in the right place.

3 Now, repeat, but after the first move horizontally, as the other outside ball is peaking, drop the dummy and snatch the peaking ball from the air. Now complete the reversal in direction. You have now swapped the original dummy for the other outside ball.

4 The action continues in the same manner and when executed correctly suggests a machine-like movement.

Snatching or Clawing

This is a method for catching balls, rather than a pattern. Instead of waiting for a ball to land in your hand, you reverse your hand and "snatch" the ball from the air.

Tip

● This is an awkward movement after practicing so long at keeping your hands in the correct place. Try this first with your stronger hand, rather than your weaker.

1 Begin with a cascade pattern. When you are comfortable, rather than waiting for a specific ball to land in your hand, reach out and snatch it from the air, just after it peaks at about eye level. Drop your hand back down to normal and launch the ball back into the cascade. By catching the ball early, you will make up for the time needed to drop your hand back down.

2 When you have tried this a few times with each hand, try a double, snatching one, then another, from the air. Eventually you will be able to snatch continuously, altering the timing and speed of the snatch to impress your audience.

Body Bouncing

Like balancing, bouncing balls off various parts of your body can be used to good effect to enhance the visual impact of your performance. As with balancing, various different parts of the body may be used.

Begin a cascade pattern. As one ball drops toward your hand, don't catch it, but raise your knee to meet the ball, using sufficient force to send it back up along a normal trajectory. This may take quite some practice, as not only do you have to "aim" the ball with your knee – which is not used to this action – but also gauge the force required to keep the ball in the pattern. The same technique can be used for either the inside or outside of your foot.

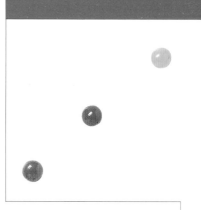

1 An alternative is to hit or tap the ball with your hand, rather than catching it.

2 Or to use the forearm in a similar manner. Both these are relatively easy as the arm is well used to the actions involved.

Body Bouncing

For the real extroverts, we'll leave you with an advanced move. During a standard cascade, leave yourself some extra time and toss one ball over the same shoulder as the hand tossing the ball, but toward the opposite foot. As it falls, raise that leg smartly backward, kicking the ball back up with the sole of your foot. The aim must be for it to peak over the same shoulder as the foot that kicked it (i.e. the opposite shoulder from the one it went over) in order to continue the cascade. Pause in your timing of throwing the other two balls so that the back-kicked ball is fully reincorporated into the cascade pattern. Not only does this need a high level of accuracy, it also needs an area completely clear of breakable objects in which to practice it.

3 And the head can be used as well. The timing needs to be sorted out as you will be "catching" the ball earlier than normal and the head is not used to performing the actions, but it is an effective bounce. Try putting all these three bounces into one sequence and you will get an idea of how effective a visual entertainment body-bouncing is.

Mill's Mess

This is one of the most difficult and spectacular of three-ball tricks. It is at first complicated and seemingly impossible to learn. As we have never found a really good instruction on this pattern, we decided that it was a perfect implementation of our "virtual video" – where we can both show you and tell how it is done. If at first you don't succeed, give it a rest for a while and then come back a little later. You will find it worth all the effort in the end.

Tip

● **This pattern is a very fluid motion, so try from the very beginning to make your actions as smooth as you can.**

1 Take one ball. Cross your hands with the ball-holding arm underneath the other. Toss this vertically straight up.

2 As it reaches its peak, uncross your arms and catch the ball with your other hand. Now cross your arms in an exact mirror of the position you started in, with the ball still held in place, and repeat the exercise in reverse. Continue to practice this move.

Mill's Mess

Key Stage

3 Take two balls, one in each hand. Position with crossed arms as before. Toss the first ball vertically as stage one and as it peaks, and before you uncross your arms, toss the second ball in a cascade movement toward your other hand. This will seem awkward as it is a sort of reverse movement from this hand.

4 Now uncross your arms. Catch Ball One in one hand.

5 And immediately recross your hands as previous exercise and catch Ball Two in the other hand (this hand is on top). You should now have one ball in each hand again. Practice this several times and starting with alternate hands.

 6 Now for Ball Three, but don't worry as the most difficult moves have already been practiced. Take two balls in one hand and one in the other. The two balls will of course be in the starting hand.

7 Ball One is thrown vertically and Ball Two in the "reverse" cascade movement.

8 Uncross your hands, collect Ball One and as Ball Two is peaking, throw Ball Three in the same trajectory as you did Ball Two.

Mill's Mess

9 Cross your arms (carrying Ball One) and catch Balls Two and Three with arms in crossed position. Stop. Now repeat this exercise.

10 You have probably guessed by now that that is all there is to it. The Mill's Mess is just the actions you have already done, but in a continuous movement. The effect, just to make sure you have it in mind, is that two balls follow each other back and forth in a snakelike move across the pattern, while the third ball climbs vertically on each side of the pattern on alternate moves. You should try to be as accurate as possible, such that the pattern leaps out of your juggling.

After you have repeated it, just run through the motions again, comparing your positions against each photograph, just to ensure you have it correct. Now rearrange yourself to do the same exercise, starting with your other hand. Repeat with both hands until you are completely comfortable with the action.

● The linkage between the two exercises you have completed is the vertical throw. Commencing from side one, carry through the exercise and then, rather than stopping as we did previously, the ending position becomes the starting position for the next set of throws, the first ball being once again thrown vertically, but on the opposite side to where you started.

Brilliant! Well done indeed! Now find a friend or family member and show off. Don't forget to take a bow when you have finished, and try passing a hat around just to see what it feels like.

Stealing and Passing

To really appreciate any particular activity, it has to be shared. For the solo juggler, the best way to share their enjoyment of juggling is to perform, to friends or to an audience. But an alternative is to juggle with a friend – or more than one if you are so lucky.

Most people when they think of juggling with someone else automatically think of passing, and club passing in particular. But perish the thought that we should be so restrictive. A fun way to start this experience is with balls, and rather than complicate matters with lots of them, let's start with just three. The technique is known as "stealing," as the idea is for one person to commence juggling and for the other to "steal" the balls and continue without breaking the pattern.

Stealing

Take three balls and a close friend. Stand facing each other, about an arm length apart. One person begins juggling a cascade. As one ball peaks, the opposing partner reaches out and snatches it. As the next peaks, snatch that as well with the other hand. Now, as the third ball peaks, toss the first (stolen) ball under it and resume the cascade. The third ball, rather than being stolen, is allowed by the first partner to fall into the second partner's pattern.

The positions may now be reversed and the balls stolen back by the original partner – and of course kept going for as long as you like.

But, as we said, most people think of passing clubs, so this is what we will now concentrate on. Do bear in mind that the techniques we are about to impart can be equally applied to balls, knives, and rings as well as to clubs, so use whatever you prefer.

So who should you work with? Of course, it is handy if you have one or more friends who also have the juggling "bug." If not, then a trip to the local juggling or circus-skills class or workshop should bring you into contact with any number of like-minded individuals. And if your area is lacking in such things, then surely this is a great opportunity to start a club.

Passing

At this point, we should make mention of skill standards and safety. First, if you're contemplating club passing, you should be very comfortable with both your own and your partner's solo skills. It is not necessary to be of a professional standard, but bearing in mind that a fairly standard club will weigh in something around half a pound of hard plastic, it will help to calm fears if everyone concerned is a capable juggler. We should also make the point that passing is also a very good improver technique, helping out solo skills in such areas as timing and throw accuracy.

The Basic Club Pass

1 The most basic move is conducted with each of the participants juggling a Three-club Cascade. The only difference to the basic cascade is that at some point in the pattern, you pass one club to your partner, receiving one from him or her in return. As may be expected, this is the difficult part, so let's start with this.

2 The hold for club passing is broadly similar to the standard hold. Try not to alter it too much as you will not find sufficient time during the routine to adjust your hands a great deal.

The Basic Club Pass

3 Stand so that you and your partner are facing each other and about 10 feet apart. Take one club and throw it to your partner, such that he (or she) catches it in the opposite hand to yours – i.e. your right hand to their left or vice versa.

4 The club should be thrown so that it executes one and a half revolutions and is caught by the receiver at about shoulder height with the club approximately vertical, rather than allowing it to drop to hand.

5 The power for the club throw comes mainly from the swing of the arm. Put in too much wrist action and the club will spin too much – they are designed to rotate naturally, and at about the 10-feet mark should quite happily perform the one and a half rotations we need.

This action has to be practiced exhaustively between the participants, with both parties able to throw and receive with either arm. Ensure that the action is kept as gentle as possible.

6 When you are comfortable with the throw, take just three clubs and one person commence a cascade. Choose a club and when it falls to hand, toss it to your partner and continue to juggle the remaining two clubs. On receipt of your club, your partner should commence the cascade pattern with a single club.

Tips

● This all sounds so complicated in theory, but you will find that the timing is more natural than many of the club tricks you have learned previously. Keep practicing until the action is smooth and remember that the point of the exercise is not just to perfect the throw/catch, but to continue the juggling pattern as well.

● While this is the way we recommend you learn, it is not necessarily the easiest route. If you find this is too difficult, move on to the next stage – five-club passing. Try that and then come back to this stage as the preface to six-club work.

Tip

● If you experience trouble with this action, try adjusting your grip. A move further toward the handle will give extra leverage and more spins, while a move away from the grip will slow the spin rate down.

The Basic Club Pass

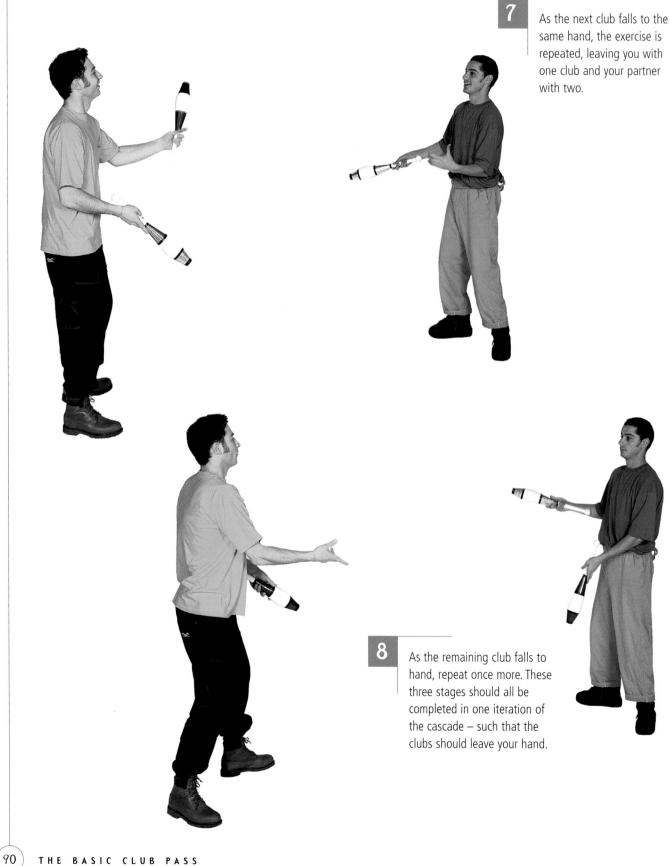

7 As the next club falls to the same hand, the exercise is repeated, leaving you with one club and your partner with two.

8 As the remaining club falls to hand, repeat once more. These three stages should all be completed in one iteration of the cascade — such that the clubs should leave your hand.

Five-club Passing

In passing, it is imperative that both parties use the same timing. Therefore you should count – out loud – as you juggle. Some tutors believe that only one hand should be counted on, but this we think is overly complex. Count each throw as you throw it.

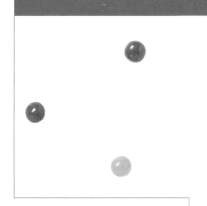

1 One person starts with three clubs, the other with two (one in each hand). The person with three clubs commences with whichever hand they feel most comfortable with. As the first club is tossed, start counting.

2 The seventh throw should be made to your partner, who should start to juggle as you count "seven." They should commence with the club in their receiving hand – and start counting again from "one." The person who threw the club should then cease juggling, one club in each hand.

Five-club Passing

3 The person juggling should then make their sixth (not seventh) throw back to the first person, who should commence juggling on the count "six." Repeat for as long as you can, then reverse directions, throwing and catching with your alternate hands.

Before you progress beyond this point, make sure that you are fully conversant with both the previous sections. If you passed over the Basic-club Pass, now is the time to go back to it and practice until you can keep up the flow of the pattern, from one to another at least five times in a row. More are preferable, but you will get more practice in the next section.

Six-club Passing

The key to passing any object is synchronization, which is where the audible count comes in. The Six-club and the Five-club Pass just practiced are made easier by not having to continue to juggle once you have passed the club(s). In six-club passing, it is a continuous movement, so timing becomes crucial.

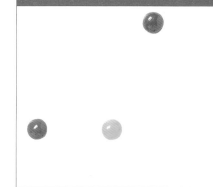

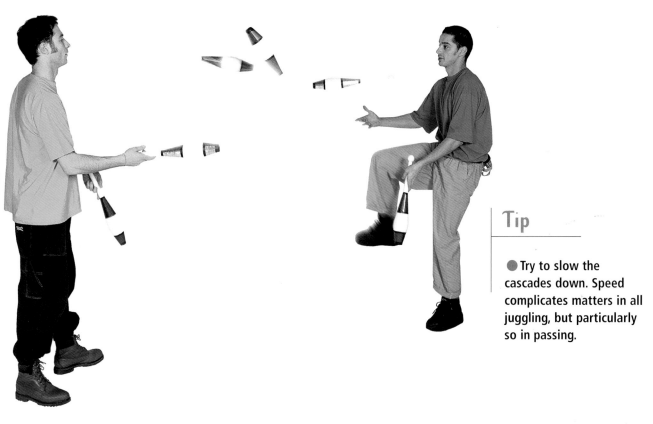

Tip

● Try to slow the cascades down. Speed complicates matters in all juggling, but particularly so in passing.

1 Take three clubs each, face each other and commence a cascade pattern. Both parties should start juggling from the same hand – i.e. either both right or both left. Count as you juggle, and stop on "ten." Do not try to pass – this exercise is to insure that the pace of both jugglers is the same, so you should both catch the last club at the same time. Practice this until timing is correct.

2 Now begin the exercise again, but this time you are going to pass. The club you begin to juggle with is the one which is going to be passed – using the same timing as for the Five-club Pass. On the count of "seven," throw your club to your partner. They will also throw theirs to you on the same count, so as the eighth club leaves your hand, it will leave it free to collect the incoming club, which will become your tenth throw. Stop here.

If everything has gone right, you should both be in a position where you have passed a club to your partner, received one back, and continued the pattern. If it has not gone right, you need to pick up the clubs you have dropped and start again.

Six-club Passing

3 Practice this exercise until you can achieve this pattern consistently. Then the idea is to continue the pattern indefinitely(!), passing every sixth throw, as with five-club passing, but both participants continue with their cascade as they also receive a club each time they pass one.

There is an alternative method to the one we have just explained. Known as the "fast start," it is a little more difficult than the first method, so if it doesn't work for you, do not be overly concerned. Go back to the original and try a few more of that.

It starts with three clubs as before, but the first throw is a pass to your partner. In order that the timing here works, you need to toss the second throw into the cascade pattern promptly, in order to leave that hand free to collect the pass from your partner. From here on, the timing is as above, with every sixth throw

passed. This method is used extensively by the professionals for the main reason that the baseline for timing is easily set on the first throw.

A further variation to try is known as "showering." This is a lot faster, so accuracy is even more vital. Begin with the "fast start" as above, but instead of waiting for each sixth throw, pass a club to your partner every third throw. This is a lot more difficult than it sounds, so do not be put off. After mastering this, you will be very confident about your passing abilities – as well as confident in your partner.

Passing Techniques and Tricks

There are a number of (non-violent) ways in which the club may be passed to a partner. The actions involved include those normal to solo juggling – differing heights, double or triple spinning, or from behind the back or under the leg – but there are also some unique to passing, such as bouncing off the floor (try it!). However you throw, remember that timing is vital as is communication with your partner – whether as audible advice of your intention or a prearranged sequence. There is absolutely no point in executing a perfect triple spinning pass over your shoulder if, as it arrives at your partner, he still has two clubs in that hand. Whatever your methods of communication with your partner, prepare to be flexible and watch the timing to make the entire pattern flow smoothly. Also beware the unexpected. If you or your partner drops a club, continue your pattern and do not pass any further clubs until the other has retrieved the offending item and has regained the correct timing to fit the pattern.

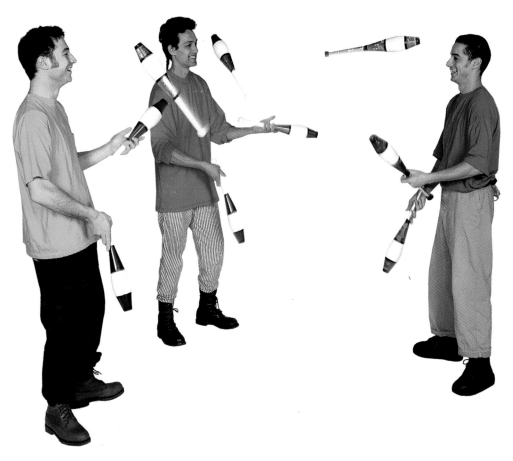

Under the Leg

1 A simple, but effective variation to a standard pass. The timing does not change from a standard pass. Instead, as you go to make the pass, turn slightly away from your partner, quickly lift your leg up, and pass the club underneath. You will find it easier if you alter your grip to nearer to the end of the club as this will give you a little more leverage. The club's trajectory needs to be altered slightly as you will be throwing from slightly lower than normal.

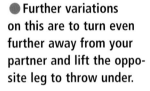

Tips

● **The higher you raise your leg, the less the effect will be on the trajectory, so try to raise it sufficiently at first that the standard throw can be maintained.**

● **Further variations on this are to turn even further away from your partner and lift the opposite leg to throw under.**

Through the Legs

1 This is another variation on Under the Leg, but is a more advanced move, due to the alterations in timing required. The throw is executed in similar fashion to the Under the Leg, but goes through the legs instead. Of course, this means you cannot raise the leg in order to reduce the impact on the trajectory and you will also be leaning backwards slightly in order to reach down, and this will put you off balance. Try practicing with a single club first of all.

Double-Spin Passes

With a normal pass, the club will naturally complete one and a half revolutions and any more than that will take more time to reach your partner and therefore impact on the timing of the entire pattern. But double spins are as visually attractive in passing as they are in their solo counterpart, so we must add them to our repertoire.

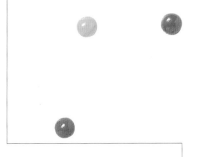

1 To throw a double which does not impact on the timing of the overall pattern, the throw needs to be across the pattern from right hand to right hand.

The arc needs to be higher than normal to allow time for the extra spin and a little extra "wrist" needs to be input to help it along.

Tip

● **Double spins are best executed at a reasonably slow pace. The accuracy of the trajectory is the key, rather than the correct number of spins. Remember, a club will turn naturally of its own accord, so don't hurry it.**

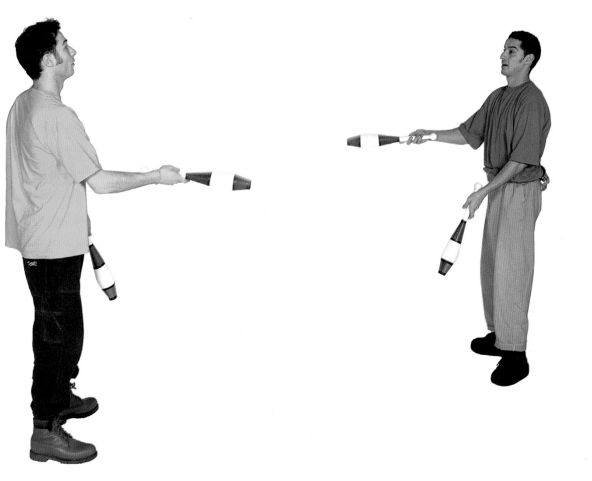

Double-Spin Passes

2 A left-hand-to-left-hand pass is quite different. In this case, accept an incoming single spin from your partner and immediately toss it in a double to your partner's left hand – again higher than normal. This effectively bypasses your right hand completely.

Triple-Spin Passes

Triple spinning requires a good deal of "feel" to the timing and wrist actions. The throw is launched immediately following the previous right-handed pass, and will require a slight pause as each partner waits for the incoming club to reach them.

Torpedo Throws (or Zero Spin)

If you are having a hard time coming to grips with spinning, try throwing one without a spin at all.

1 This pass is a standard right-to-left pass, but the club needs to be spun through just half a turn and then travel flat as it travels through the air. The technique is not as simple as the description – as the club is passed, you need to be holding it further up toward the body and push it away from you toward your partner (this action is similar to throwing a dart). The effectiveness of this trick is enhanced if both partners execute it simultaneously.

Passing With More Than Two People

There are as many ways to juggle between people as there are people to juggle with. There is no limitation to the number who can join in: it just takes that much more communication. There is, however, one technique that needs to be practiced and understood, which will give you an indication of how to progress further. It is known as the "feed."

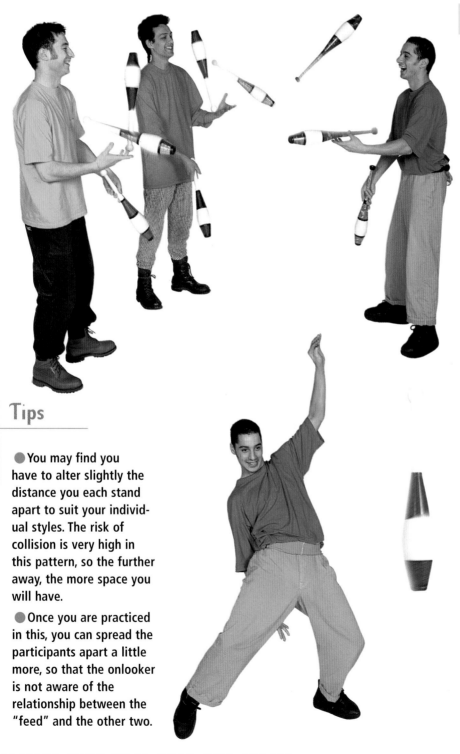

Two people stand side by side, with one person opposite. The single person should be the most competent of the three and acts as the "feed." As the three participants commence juggling with standard timing, the "feed" alternates passing with one of the other two in turn. If this is carried out turn and turn about, then, while from an onlooker's point of view it looks like continuous passing, it is only the feed who is passing continuously – each of the other two passes only every other time.

Tips

● You may find you have to alter slightly the distance you each stand apart to suit your individual styles. The risk of collision is very high in this pattern, so the further away, the more space you will have.

● Once you are practiced in this, you can spread the participants apart a little more, so that the onlooker is not aware of the relationship between the "feed" and the other two.

CHAPTER 6
Other Juggling Items

Other than balls and clubs, there are a myriad of other objects which can be juggled. The Devil, or Rhythm, Stick is a weighted and shaped wooden baton which is juggled using two smaller pieces of dowel, or hand sticks. It is designed to be spun, tossed and generally thrown around creating an impressive air dance which in many respects seems to defy gravity. The idea came across to the Western world from China a couple of centuries ago, brought, as were so many other Eastern influences, by missionaries.

The Diabolo is thought to have originated about the same time, from the same source. Looking rather like a large yo-yo, it is not attached to a string, but is controlled by a separate string attached to a couple of hand sticks. The leverage that this system enjoys, means that a high rate of spin can be achieved, giving the Diabolo incredible stability through the gyroscopic-type forces operating through it. Not only can it be tossed and passed like a devil stick, but the string can be used to weave it into intricate and visually stunning patterns.

Devil Sticks

The basic art of the Devil Stick is to tap it between the two hand sticks such that it describes an arc just in front of your chest. This is known as "double-sticking."

1 The easiest way to start and get a good feel for your stick is to kneel or crouch holding it just in front of you, with one end resting on the ground around 18 inches in front of your knees. Hold the hand sticks naturally in each hand and, holding one horizontally in front of you, rest the Devil Stick against it.

Devil Sticks

4 Progress to standing up and practice the basic double-stick-ing until you are quite happy with the movement and can keep the Devil Stick consistently airborne.

2 Hold your other hand stick parallel to the first and at shoulder's width and tap the Devil Stick from one to the other, leaving it in contact with the ground at the base. The tap should be more of a push than a thwack. The point of contact should be three-quarters up the Devil Stick and approximately half to two-thirds of the way down the hand stick.

3 After a few minutes, practice, you are ready to lift the Devil Stick from the ground. The action is to lift and toss the stick from one hand stick to the other. From the earlier exercise, rather than just tap-ping the Devil Stick, impart a little "lift" into your tap and

you will notice that the Devil Stick lifts off the floor. When it reaches the other stick, do not just "whack" it back, but let it rest on your hand stick for a split second (absorb the momentum with "give" in your wrist), before tapping it back – again with "lift."

Tip

● **Keep the hand sticks roughly horizontal and parallel – do not let your hand let them splay apart as this will result in the Devil Stick moving forward, making you reach or move.**

1 Once you have started double-sticking from the floor a few times, you may like to start with an alternative, which does not require kneeling on the floor. From a standing position, hold your hand sticks parallel and rest the Devil Stick on top of them.

2 Simply remove one hand stick, letting the Devil Stick fall, and, as it does, give it a lift and push with the remaining hand stick. From this position, it is simply a method of commencing double-sticking.

Try to keep the movement slow and even. If you find yourself tapping faster and faster, you are holding your hands too close together and not hitting the Devil Stick hard enough.

If the Devil Stick tries to roll over your hand stick, you are hitting it too low and need to adjust your contact point further toward the top of the stick.

As with other types of juggling, count how many times you can repeat the exercise and try to better yourself each time. Try to develop a consistent rhythm.

Spins and Double Spins

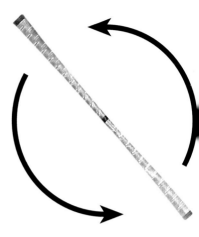

A spin is achieved by purely imparting a harder tap/push to the Devil Stick during normal double-sticking and allowing it to spin completely around before "catching" it with the other hand stick. It is a slight misnomer, in that it is actually one and a quarter turns, rather than a single spin.

Double spins need an even harder push. Like multispins in club juggling, one of the most common reasons to throw spins in Devil Sticking, is to gain time — either to adjust position or to permit the time to set up for a more complex maneuver to follow.

Windmill

A Windmill is achieved by catching the Devil Stick just below the center point instead of the normal three-quarter point. The stick will then continue to rotate over the hand stick, rather than being pushed back. Now move the hand stick in a circular fashion, following the movement of the Devil Stick, but using the hand stick to keep it relatively in the same position. After one revolution, catch it with the other hand stick in the normal fashion and continue double-sticking.

For a continuous windmill movement, maintain pressure on the Devil Stick while moving the hand stick in a circular fashion.

Whirlpool Spins

1 The Whirlpool Spin is conducted around a different plane from what we have done so far – the Devil Stick revolves in a horizontal rather than vertical plane. Start by double sticking as before, but more slowly. As the Devil Stick rests for a millisecond on one hand stick, allow it to balance and just push forward with the stick. The effect of this is that the Devil Stick begins to revolve in the horizontal plane. As it comes around, catch it on the other stick, and as it balances, pull the hand stick toward you. Continue the movement by alternately pushing and pulling.

2 The Whirlpool Spin can also be maintained, once begun, with one stick. As the whirlpool movement is established, use a single stick to push and pull on each side. As the point of contact with the Devil Stick is very close to the center point, the amount of movement by the one hand holding the hand stick is quite small.

Single Sticking

This is a variation on double sticking, using just the one hand stick. Establish a double-sticking movement, but, instead of using the alternate hand stick, swiftly move the same hand across and tap back using a "backhand" movement. Practice this with each hand.

Again, you will find that throwing a single spin each time will give you the additional time to move your hand across. The trick looks most effective without spinning, so once you are happy with the basic move, cut out the spin.

Under the Leg

1 This trick is very effective, and not as hard as it seems. Throw a single spin for time and in that time lift your opposite leg. Reach under your leg with that hand stick and catch and toss the Devil Stick back again. Practice this several times until you are consistent with each leg.

Behind the Back

1 This, as you can see is a slight misnomer in that the Devil Stick is not actually behind the back, but to the side, with one hand passed behind the back and the other held out to one side. Throw a double spin, and in the extra time, turn your body around not quite half a turn, whipping one hand behind your back to insure that you still have two sticks available. Catch the Devil Stick with one stick and continue to double-stick – although now the action is "backhanded," rather than the normal action.

The Diabolo

Due to the way it appears to an onlooker, one of the most common fallacies with the Diabolo is that it reverses in direction in the same way as does a yo-yo. the practitioner moves his hands alternately up and down and, for all the world, this is the impression it gives. In fact, nothing is further from the truth ...

1   Stand loosely at ease. Take the string and hand sticks and let the string lie on the ground, put your Diabolo in front of you on the ground, midway between your feet and covering the string.

Tip

● For the sake of good order, try to keep the Diabolo in the same position to you. Adjust your position to keep it in the center of your body. The following additional tips will help if this leaves you with your back to the audience.

2 Holding the hand sticks together, pull them toward one side so that the Diabolo rolls along the ground. We assume for the purposes of the lesson that it moves from left to right.

3 As you stand without moving, the Diabolo will reach a point where it naturally lifts off the ground. As it does, move the hand sticks apart and let your left hand drop, while simultaneously jerking the right hand upward. The effect of this should be that the string, slackened by dropping your left hand, does not have any effect of the spin on the Diabolo.

4 Now lift your left hand with a pulling motion, while allowing your right hand to maintain the grip of the string on the Diabolo – although it will have to move downward in order to keep the Diabolo relatively in the same place. The effect of this move is to impart greater spin on the Diabolo.

5 Continue these two moves alternately. The cumulative effect is to keep the Diabolo spinning in the same direction as when you pulled it across the floor.

Tips

● If the Diabolo begins to tilt toward you, maintain the pull with the hand sticks, but move the right-hand stick away from your body. Similarly if it begins to tilt away from you, move the left-hand stick away from you, or pull the right-hand stick toward you.

● Once you are well practiced, these correction movements, like so many others in juggling, will become automatic.

6 Once a reasonable amount of spin has been achieved, hold your hands still at the same level and watch how the Diabolo maintains its balance. This is the crux of Diabolo – it is the same forces acting to keep the Diabolo upright as keep you upright on a bicycle.

The Diabolo

7 Most people associate Diabolos with throwing and catching. The very first maneuver most people want to learn once the basics have been practiced is to toss the Diabolo in the air. First get the Diabolo spinning regularly, then, letting the Diabolo rest in the "V," pull the hand sticks apart with a movement hard enough to propel the Diabolo into the air. You will find that this is best achieved if you insure that the string is taut between the hand sticks.

8 But what goes up must come down. Catching the Diabolo is achieved by just keeping the string taut and under the trajectory of the descending Diabolo. As it touches the string, absorb the weight by bringing the hand sticks together and continue to maintain the spin. You will find that it is much easier to catch the Diabolo once greater heights are achieved by raising one hand above your eye line and in line with the descending object, while keeping the string taut with the other hand, slightly lower. The raised hand will then be brought down at a great speed than the lower in order that they be level once the Diabolo is back to its standard position.

Fast Spinning

In order for the Diabolo to maintain its balance during advanced tricks – many of which take time to complete – it has to be spun very quickly.

There are two techniques to achieve this, both of which will require some practice to get right.

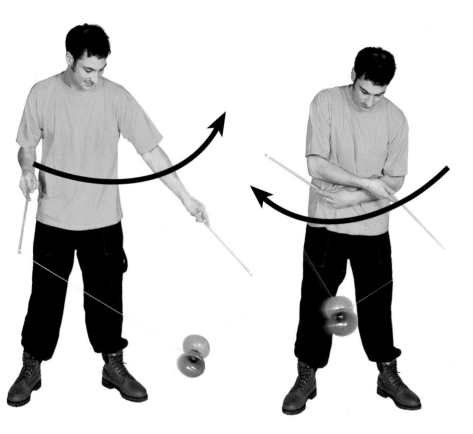

Tips

● Each alternate "whip" must be behind the other hand, as otherwise the Diabolo will begin to tilt. At first, you will probably whip the right hand back to uncross either too early or too late, resulting in an unbalanced Diabolo. This is normal until you get the "feel" for the correct timing.

1 From a standard spin, move your right arm out from your body, letting your left arm move across toward it, then whip your right hand completely across your body, resulting in a crossed arm position.

2 The Diabolo will follow the movement. As it reaches the end and begins to pull, whip your hand back to the starting position and repeat the action, but with the right hand moving behind the left. This action is repeated continuously until the desired spin speed is achieved.

The alternative action is that, while spinning the Diabolo normally, let the string slacken and quickly loop the string an extra time around the axle. You may now jerk the hand sticks with greater vigor without the Diabolo leaping out of control. Do not overspin your Diabolo at very high speeds.

Imperfections in control or balance of the Diabolo will work against it and it will lose balance. Once the desired rate of spin is achieved, remember to take out the loop before attempting the trick.

Around the World

2 Once a complete circle has been described, continue the movement so that the Diabolo swings down past the opposite foot, up behind that shoulder and over your head (the complete reverse of the first movement).

1 Spin the Diabolo normally, and, once balance has settled, hold the hand sticks closely together, swinging the Diabolo over your hands in a circular motion and then down toward your right foot, up behind your shoulder and over your head.

3 Then, as the Diabolo complete its second loop to arrive in front of you, turn the hand sticks in toward each other and flick your wrists outward so that the Diabolo loops in toward your stomach and the up and over the hand sticks. This completes the trip "Around the World" and leave the strings completely untwisted and the Diabolo ready to b spun up for the next trick.

Foot Tapper

This is a delightful, almost "throwaway" movement, which usually leaves onlookers wondering exactly what they saw. Drop both your hands, so that the Diabolo is closer to the ground than normal. Lift your foot and, holding your hands apart and quite steady, tap the string with the front part of your foot, just a little to the side of the Diabolo. The Diabolo will leap over your foot, landing on the string the other side. Swiftly move your foot back out of the way.

This trick can be extended with practice to a Leg Jumper. In this trick, the leg is bent at the knee, such that the entire leg is over the string. The string is then tapped with the foot with sufficient force for the Diabolo to be propelled up and over the knee, rather than just the foot.

Tip

● You will find it easier if the hand stick on the side that the foot is tapping is held just a little lower than the other.

Some additional practice will then lead you to raise the stakes once more and try the Hiphopper.

Reverse/Cross Catch

Tip

● If you find you are having problems catching in this position, try raising one hand stick above your eye level and in line with the descending Diabolo.

Not only is this a little trick in its own right, but it is also the starting position of the Cat's Cradle. Toss the Diabolo and then, before you catch it, cross your arms. To get out of this, simply toss the Diabolo once more – still with your arms crossed – and uncross your arms before catching.

Cat's Cradle

This is a beautiful trick when it is presented well. Visually complicated, it is in fact not too difficult to master.

Tip

● **Practice the loose cradle without the Diabolo. Cross your arms, pull the right-hand stick across the middle of the other, leaving a loop which you then "knit" the right-hand stick through. Pull the hand sticks apart to tighten the string.**

1 First, ensure the Diabolo is spinning quickly, then toss it up and cross your arms before catching (reverse/cross catch). Uncross your lower (left) hand, which will pull the string of the right stick out, then the other (right) stick is "knitted" into the center of the two strings and pulled outward as the arms complete the uncrossing motion.

2 You are now in the loose cradle position. From this position, toss up the Diabolo once more and as it leaves the string, pull the hand sticks apart to leave the string taut.

3 Catch the Diabolo in the "V" created by the Cat's Cradle. Pause for effect/applause. Then just turn the tips of the hand sticks inward and drop your hands, and the Diabolo will just drop out of the cradle utilizing its own momentum, leaving you back at the standard position.

Monkey Climb

1 Like many Diabolo moves, this one is very easy to explain, but will require a good deal of practice before it is consistently achieved. Loop the Diabolo and get it spinning really quite quickly. Leave the cord looped and raise the left hand stick up to about eye level.

2 Gently pull down the right hand stick and the Diabolo will appear to "climb" the string in direct contravention of gravity – and probably most state-laws! If at first you succeed with this trick, you will be in a minority, as it takes a good deal of expertise in the amount of tension required in the string, as well as ensuring that sufficient spin speed is obtained before the climb attempt is made.

Over the Top

This is an extremely pretty little trick which will give you some indication of what you can achieve with the Diabolo. With the Diabolo spinning quite normally, hold the left hand stick steady, laying the string of the right hand stick against the mid-part of the left. In one fluid movement, swing the Diabolo inward and over the top of the left hand stick, by pushing the right hand stick over and down. As the right hand stick pulls through back to its normal position, the left follows over and also back to its normal position.

High Wire

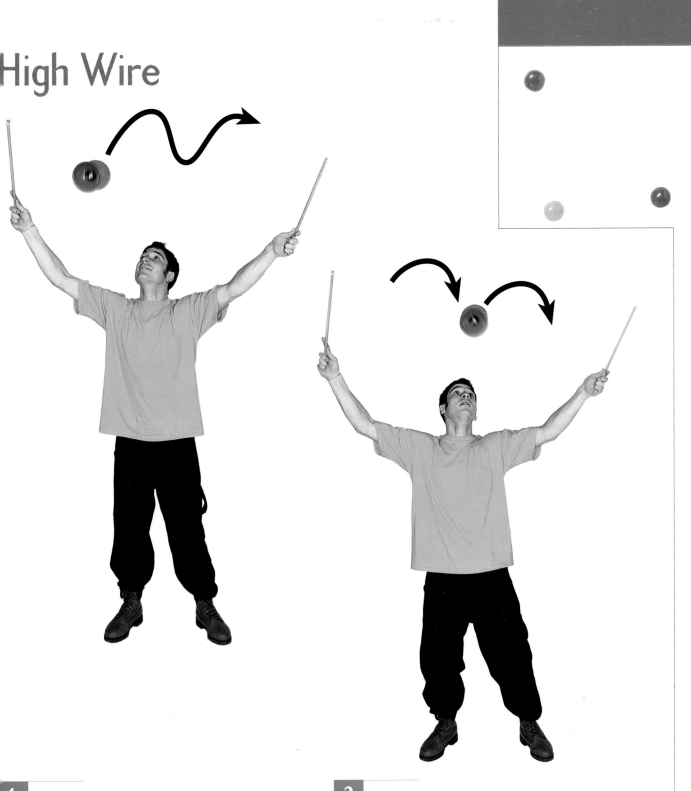

1 This trick requires a fast spin. When this is achieved, raise your hands above your head, keeping your hands level and pulling them apart to keep the string taut.

2 By loosening the hand sticks a little, and pulling them quickly but gently apart again, you will be able to "bounce" the Diabolo along the string like a tightrope walker moving along the wire.

Flash Finish

Now that you have mastered the Diabolo, you need something to finish off your performance. This is a good way to end.

1 Throw the Diabolo quite high, allowing yourself time to adjust the hand sticks while it is in the air. Gather both the sticks in your stronger hand and position them so that they form a "V" shape (ignore the string – just let it dangle). As the Diabolo falls, catch it in the center of the "V" to a huge burst of spontaneous applause from your audience – if they don't respond immediately, remind them of the definition of the word "spontaneous" (arising from an unforced personal impulse; voluntary; unpremeditated)!

CHAPTER 7
Equipment

Balls

Earlier, we described the best type of balls for learning with. These are not the only type of ball and indeed are not the ones most favored by experienced jugglers. Most jugglers prefer balls that can bounce, not necessarily because they want to bounce them, but because that particular attribute can be very useful – not least if you drop one accidentally.

The very best juggling balls are made of silicone. These will give a consistent bounce and feel good to the touch – juggling for a long time can become painful if the balls have a seam or are uneven to the touch. Tennis balls are not recommended as they are too light for good control. Any hard rubber ball will be good – for example, a lacrosse ball.

Then there are balls that glow in the dark. Mainly, these are of the luminous type, which have varying degrees of a luminous chemical added to the material as they are made. After you hold them up to a light source, they will glow for some while in the dark. There are also battery-powered balls, which contain small, colored LEDs (light-emitting diodes), the benefit of which is that they glow for considerably longer than the luminous type. They are, however, much more expensive, both to buy and to keep fed with batteries.

There are two types of fire balls (yes, really). One type is commercially made of a spiral of thick metal wire, encasing a center axle containing the wick. The other type tends to be hand-made of wood, with a wick wrapped around it.

Asbestos, or at the very least some sturdy flame-resistant gloves, are recommended additional equipment before you try these out: the flame may not hurt so much, as the balls are not in your hand for very long, but both the metal and the wooden versions conduct the heat into all their surfaces, making it uncomfortable without protection.

The serious juggler will want to have a ball that will fit nicely in the palm. For stage work, a slightly larger one is advisable as it makes it more visible to the audience.

For those of you with leanings toward health and fitness, you can even get very large balls weighing 2 lb and more – juggling with these for any length of time will certainly help with fitness training.

Clubs

There are clubs to suit every sort of personal preference and pocket, for this is what it amounts to. The cheaper clubs are one-piece molded plastic and may be decorated or plain. As we saw earlier, modern manufacturing techniques are sufficiently advanced to be able to make a very high-quality, balanced club from a one-piece molding and we can unreservedly recommend these for both beginner and improver.

Serious jugglers still seem to prefer a two-piece club, although whether this is due to a real, as opposed to imaginary, benefit is hard to tell. Two-piece clubs have historically held the high ground and it will probably be many years before a well-made one-piece is as acceptable to the professional.

Part of the problem lies with the handle and the comfort factor. Juggling for many hours a day puts pressure on the hands of a juggler and, the more comfortable the grip, the happier the juggler. Certainly it is the case that many one-piece clubs have a broader and much harder grip than the usual two-piece.

Other than construction, weight is a factor that must be assessed. Light clubs are not advised for beginners as they are more difficult to control – even though the cheapest clubs on the market are often the lightest as they contain less material. To begin with, avoid these at all costs – anything that makes the learning process more difficult should be shunned.

There are of course luminous clubs, which are made of a similar material to that of luminous balls, and there are fire clubs, which we deal with at the end of this chapter.

Please take note of the safety advice we give. Fire products can be very dangerous indeed.

Many jugglers like to incorporate everyday objects into their routines. Try sink plungers, which make really excellent clubs – normally very well balanced. Sticks and umbrellas may also be used. If you are intent on using knives or axes, do not on any account use the real thing – professionals use specially made juggling props which look extremely lifelike but are completely blunt and impossible to cut oneself with.

Devil Sticks

Most Devil Sticks are thin at the middle and flared gently outward toward the tips, which are then protected with a rubber covering. These give the best weight and balance characteristics. Generally, professional hand sticks are covered with silicone – which of course is easily the most expensive material – but very good-quality sticks are to be found that are coated with a specially tacky form of latex. Silicone tends to be a see-through, white color, while most latex is black. The sticky latex versions can be had in most colors, which is an additional benefit of this material. Best avoided are taped sticks, as these are unlikely to grip very well and will make the Devil Stick more difficult to control.

Various attempts have been made over the years to construct a Devil Stick of a material other than wood, but almost no other material has the amount of flexibility that will permit a stick to survive the impact with the floor that most Devil Sticks experience in use. For this reason, you will not see a luminous stick, although fire versions are available.

Flower Sticks

These are another form of Devil Stick, but with an addition of a tassle on each end. The theory is that the tassle will slow down the spin speed of the standard Devil Stick and permit an easier learning curve. The second theory is that the tassle adds to the visual impact. While we can see some evidence for the former, we encourage you to use the best-balanced and best-weighted stick that you can, as the speed is secondary to the quality of the product. As for the latter theory, we suggest that it is the skill utilized that really shows off the product, not the stick itself.

Diabolos

Diabolos are generally made of either a molded plastic or latex material. The two cups are connected with an axle – usually metal – and either bolted together or pinned. The bolted version permits adjustment should the connector work its way loose over time and for this reason is to be preferred over the pin type.

The Diabolo's quality is all in the balance and this can be affected by any and all of the components, so it is important for each to be made to an exacting standard. Again, Diabolos come in a range of different styles and sizes, the larger ones being more appropriate for stage work.

Luminous and fire Diabolos are available. We have even seen a battery-powered model, but this is too difficult to balance, and too heavy to be considered a serious tool.

The hand sticks for Diabolos are not as important as for Devil Sticks, so long as they are sturdy and comfortable. Most important is how the string is tied on, as it can be very embarrassing to have it untie in the middle of an act. If you failed knots as a Boy Scout, then we recommend that you pass the string through the hole, loop it around the stick and then, after knotting it any way you like, pull the knot back through the hole so that it is held tight.

Fire Products

Juggling is a very visual exercise and jugglers like to make it more so for the better enjoyment of their audience. There is also something primeval about fire that attracts children and jugglers alike and has led to a number of standard juggling props being manufactured to be set alight – they number fire clubs, fire Devil Sticks and fire Diabolos among them.

The techniques for juggling these items are identical to juggling the standard products – you just have to be that much more careful, as anyone who has ever seen a runaway fire Diabolo will agree. We give here, for the benefit of those of you drawn to this particular field, some short tips on how to handle your equipment and some very important pieces of advice for safety.

Tips and Safety

It may rather be stating the obvious, but fire products require careful handling. First, do not attempt to work with fire products until you are extremely competent with the basic product – that is, you do not drop while juggling any of your standard tricks as a matter of course. The following pieces of advice should also be borne in mind:

● Before setting your fire product alight, juggle with it unlit until you feel comfortable with its different weight and flight characteristics.

● If you are going to be juggling with fire clubs, wear gloves and practice juggling with the gloves on and the clubs unlit until you are comfortable.

- It is a good idea to wear gloves whatever you are juggling with. They will help protect you in case of mishap.

- Only ever use kerosene. It burns well, but has a lower heat than other fluids.

- Never use denatured-alcohol products, as these burn giving off fumes and have an overly bright flame which may damage your eyes.

- To prime your equipment, immerse the wick in the kerosene for two or three seconds. Use a bowl – do not pour the kerosene over the wick.

- When you have primed your equipment, put the top back on your bottle of fluid and move it well away from the juggling area.

- Before you light the product, shake all the excess fluid off the wicks as otherwise it may "spit" over you as you light it.

- When you do first set it on fire, do it outside – avoiding windy days – in a place where it will not set fire to anything else. Just watch it for a short while to get the feel of how the flames behave.

- Check your wicks regularly and replace them if they look thin.

- On no account should you **ever** juggle fire products over or around someone else. Leave passing fire clubs to the professionals.

Anything Else at All

We mentioned sink plungers earlier in the book. You can try tennis rackets and umbrellas. As you perfect your techniques, we can add back into the equation fruit, eggs, and any type of ball. We have not covered rings, plates, or cigar boxes, but then again, neither have we covered bottles or chairs or tables. Almost anything that can be lifted can be juggled with, so let your imagination work.

As we started the book with a warning, so will we end this section: beware of small children and breakable objects. Juggling is a fun pastime, but that fun is irreparably spoiled through injury or breakage. Juggle safely!

CHAPTER 8

Performing

People juggle for different reasons: personal challenge, relaxation, stress relief, or for the entertainment of others. Certainly throughout the book so far we have stressed the "show-off" element as being something to drive you forward.

While it is true that there are introspective jugglers, there are also a great number who are extroverts, wanting to show off their art – often for reward as well as simple pleasure. This section is dedicated to helping you devise routines that are visually stimulating and entertaining from an outsider's perspective. Many of the tips included here will stand you in good stead whether you are entertaining family and friends, on a street, or on a stage.

When most people consider the term "juggler" it is normally most associated with circus, often with clowns. Within the context of circus skills, juggling is considered an art in itself and is well practiced as both street performance and vaudeville, or cabaret. Like all performance, juggling requires constant practice, not only on the basic skills, but also on "business" – aspects such as body movement to emphasize a particular pattern or flourish, and "patter," the talk that acts as a link for the performance.

The most important point to bear in mind in con-structing a routine is that it must be appro-priate to the occasion. Do not devise one single routine and try to apply it to every circumstance you find yourself in. It is all very well working long hours perfecting a street show which includes an extremely complex pattern while commenting scathingly on the current political scene, but this will not go down well at six-year-old cousin Sarah's birthday party – when an enormously high toss with a Diabolo will certainly impress as much! So consider your audience and what they

will enjoy as well as what you will enjoy showing them.

The essential tools of a good performer will include relevant or entertaining verbal material and music in addition to juggling skills. These help to create atmosphere to complement the visual performance. They are personal and everybody has their own ideas and style, so we will go no further than to stress their importance and warn, from personal experience, that a badly constructed chatter will put an audience to sleep faster than a political broadcast – often for much of the same reason!

In addition to words and music, "business" may include clapping your hands – which gives an aural as well as a visual effect – pirouettes, jumps and leg-lifting, and other body movements to accentuate the pattern being performed.

We should also include balancing within this topic. This can be utilized in two ways. One is to use one of the objects you are juggling with, where it is the alteration to the timing and pattern of your performance that is as visually stimulating as the balancing act itself. You might for instance move from a Three-club Cascade, taking one club and balancing it on your chin, while the other two clubs are pro-gressed into a Two In One Hand, and thence back to a cascade. The other form is where an additional object such as a glass of water is balanced on the head while you juggle three or more objects.

An exciting or innovative (or prefer-ably both!) balancing routine is an entrancing spectacle and will keep your audience highly entertained and enthralled.

Difficulty, insofar as an audience is concerned, lies not only with the complexity of a pattern or technique, but also with the equipment used or the situation it is being used in. Fire equipment or knives are a good example of the former of these two concepts; juggling while on a tightrope or unicycle is an example of the latter. The only limitation is the mind's ability to consider various ways of putting a performance together, although the performer's own abilities should not be overlooked!

Audience participation is always a useful way of achieving a reaction from a crowd, but a word of warning – never use your skills to put down or show up an ordinary mortal. A member of an audience can be used either as a "dumb prop" to juggle around or over for example, or made to look clever by your skills in adapting timings – for example throwing in additional items to juggle with as you juggle.

Quite a lot of mileage can be got out of using unusual objects to juggle with (one famous troupe went so far as to encourage members of their audience to bring along objects with which to challenge the skill of the jugglers). A very good item is one that is edible, then in the middle of a simple Three-ball Cascade, quickly snatch the object out of the pattern and take a bite. The comedy potential of such tricks adds to their general flavor of difficulty.

Performing with a friend or colleague can be a lot of fun and lead to interaction between you, which is as engaging as the skills performed. A pair who work – and practice – together may end up "jamming" on an unrehearsed basis similar to musicians. This can be extremely entertaining as it is fresh and its vibrancy is communicated to the audience. Passing routines are great crowd-pleasers and can be varied in many ways. As you become more advanced, you can try passing with different objects – such as sink plungers – as well as trying fire clubs or knives. Just a little word of warning: passing needs a lot of practice – a club in the face hurts even when it's not on fire.

Diabolos can be quite spectacular crowd-pleasers, but more so if worked between two. Not only can the Diabolo be tossed between you, but spectacular routines can be devised as each of you "pretends" to outdo the other (while of course being fully practiced and rehearsed).

Indoor or night performance can have an added dimension to music and sound – light. With the advent of UV and battery-powered balls and clubs, not to mention fire, a fairly standard routine can be transformed into a breathtaking audio-visual experience, leaving audiences gasping with wonder.

However, and wherever, you choose to perform is entirely your concern. Above all you should enjoy it. There is a show-off inside us all, so exploit this characteristic for all it is worth. We wish you much happiness and as much reward as you deserve for the time, energy, and patience you put into the practice.

Happy Juggling!

The Authors

Robert Irving has worked for More Balls Than Most for three years and runs their UK operation. Although his passport describes him as an International Accountant and his wife describes him as "a typical bean counter," he is actually a very interesting person (he says) and has been juggling for over 10 years. He has just managed to grasp the Three-ball Cascade and now considers himself an expert.

Mike Martins is the head demonstrator for More Balls Than Most's corporate team. When let loose from this role he enjoys maintaining his street performance and is a regular in London's Covent Garden. He also is a leading performer in the Sci-Fi Circus Cabaret "Conspiracy" and his own performance troupe have supported such international acts as "Archaos."

Acknowledgements

We would like to thank More Balls Than Most for permission to adapt the techniques they have popularized for basic work on Three-ball and Three-club Cascade, Diabolo and Devil Stick, for various extracts from their Short Course in Life Enhancement – Vol 2, and for the loan of much of the equipment shown in the photographs.

More Balls Than Most USA
26 West 17th Street
Suite 702
New York, NY 10011

Tel: (212) 691-9660
Fax:(212) 691-9633
(from within US)

More Balls Than Most UK
PO Box 41
Rickmansworth
Herts, WD3 2BJ

Tel: 01923 492525
Fax: 01923 492599
(from within UK)

Heartfelt thanks also for help with the photography to Rob Lane, Andy Nicholls, Natasha McGhie, and Kate Mason. Baby Jess did nothing but hinder the entire shoot.